ROGER DRUITT was surrounded by Nature as a boy, growing up on a farm. Since the age of three he has wanted to understand the world, and was fortunate to meet Anthroposophy in his teens. He studied mathematics at Cambridge, graduating in Economics to work in computing. He discovered the Anthroposophical Society and The Christian Community in the 1960s and has enjoyed the inspiration of both movements ever since, teaching widely on aspects of Nature observation and connecting to the hidden spirit. Festivals have been important both in his work as a priest and that of his wife Ann's work as educator and mother. They live in Sussex and have four children, five hens, eight grandchildren and thousands of bees.

FESTIVALS OF THE YEAR

A Workbook for Re-enlivening the Christian Festive Cycle

Roger Druitt

Sophia Books

Acknowledgements:
To Ann Druitt for the idea,
Heidi Herrmann, Jean Flynn and Peter van Breda for good advice
and many others for interest and encouragement

Sophia Books
Rudolf Steiner Press
Hillside House, The Square
Forest Row, East Sussex RH18 5ES

www.rudolfsteinerpress.com

Published by Sophia Books 2014
An imprint of Rudolf Steiner Press

A catalogue record for this book is available from the British Library

ISBN 978 1 85584 392 9

Cover by Andrew Morgan Design. Candle image © Neyro
Typeset by DP Photosetting, Neath, West Glamorgan
Printed and bound by Berforts Ltd., Herts

CONTENTS

INTRODUCTION

Like any living being, the Earth needs to be given substance and sustenance. In earlier ages, she could do this through her own inherent vitality, out of her own resources. Have we not made too many assumptions, taken this for granted; until we now see her in trouble, in chaos, and now needs *us* to nourish and maintain *her*? Clearly, this can only be done from a source that is *not* within her—and of all of creation that is Man. We are nowadays considered to be a special kind of animal, but that is true only up to a point. One can demonstrate that animals display qualities of soul, including even a type of thinking, but human beings can observe and think about their own thoughts, how they connect or fail to do so. It is only we that bear this ability. I would call this faculty *spirit.* It is this simple-sounding characteristic that makes us able to stand over against nature. This shows particularly in the case of our own nature, for what other creature can change its own habits? This human spirituality can be enhanced without limit and through it human beings can access those forces from beyond nature that do *not yet* lie within her. This means something that does not originate within the creation we know can re-enliven it for the future, from beyond itself. One of the ways in which this can happen is with each festival celebration where we go beyond ourselves to become creators from beyond nature. We can follow the Christian festivals, not now as reclothed nature ones but as the stage for our own creativity.

Christianity still has its doctrines and protocol for decent living as do other religions and at their best they all contribute equally to human life. However in the three fundamental Christian festivals of Christmas, Easter and Whitsun, Christianity has the *potential* to transcend the others. Look at it like this:

> Christmas—a birth;
> Easter—a death and a renewal on a totally new level;
> Whitsun—the releasing into the whole human community of what has been thereby won out of this new creation.

If we can take Christianity as a power that embraces all three of these processes then it *reveals* its potential to re-enliven the fading forces of nature. Man, the pinnacle of nature but the least of the spirit, can turn upwards to absorb this potential, then turn back to nature to bestow it upon her. How this may be done is the purpose of what follows.

These festivals are then not merely commemorative; they become a real, creative dynamic. If we find that to be true, through the 'experimentations' of this book, we shall have perceived something of the real *power* of Christianity, as distinct from its being a 'religion of the book'.

I invite you to travel with me along the spiral of the yearly festivals, to share what I have discovered there in the 40 years I have been exploring, with many others, this path. I hope you will find a fuller feeling for your own festivals and a latent creative talent for them within your domestic or working situation. I also hope your festivals become a real link between your own spirit and the spirit that weaves through the year.

Regarding non-Christian religions

This work is written for everybody, regardless of religious persuasion. The impulse is to share directions that are new also to most representations of Christianity. All the themes are of an essentially *human* orientation, transcending doctrine. Some of them, for example Michaelmas, can readily be accessible to certain non-Christian persuasions. Judaism and Islam, for example, share the parts of the Old Testament where the Archangel Michael appears. As dragon-tamer he also appears in other religions and mythologies. At Christmas or Easter, for example, where the *Christian* orientation is quite categorical, readers are invited to see whether the descriptions cannot be used to uncover a truth in a quite different religion and bring it out in potency and revelation. It is the author's conviction that anyone conscious of their humanity and aware of their own religious persuasion, whatever it is, can find treasure in the Christian cycle of the year as it is here understood and presented.

But how can one be originally creative when the headings of these chapters bear Christian festival names? How can I be original by using a 2000-year-old system? What has Christianity to offer over other religions that make her able to show the way forward? I hope to answer this now. Many of us have for example, as adults, adopted a different diet from that of our childhood. We have chosen freely; realities of life have influenced our choice, and who feels an encroachment on their freely striving self through that? So the Christian ingredient of this book is not its doctrinal or theological content but its factual, life-giving contribution to the world's life. The background proposal is that it is just in the *festival cycle of the year* that this contribution is most accessible and can even be followed without having to abandon one's own (even non-Christian) religious practice.

Living on the Earth

Wherever we dwell upon the Earth we soon become aware of the rhythms of life. After breathing, the most personal is that of day and night, for it is related to the human need to alternate sleeping and waking in a regular way. At the other end of the scale is the rhythm of life cycles, of birth and death. We only become clearly aware of this part-way through adulthood, when we realize that life not only unfolds but also closes and fades away. Our life is like the daytime part of the rhythms of days: what corresponds to the night-time of life is unseen, yet our intuition sometimes does perceive it. And the question of repeated visits to earthly life through the gate of birth is a very topical one, the answer to which would throw light on many a modern dilemma.

Between these small and great rhythms, the rhythm of the year gradually becomes the most important one in our lives. As children we grew to mark our inner stature by the year. Each year was a major addition to our whole being, yet we looked forward eagerly to special occasions or seasons in it. The year is the vessel that holds the days, for it is the unit in which the variation of the days repeats itself; and our life is built up of the right number of years to make our earthly being complete.

As we go through the year, we want to highlight the days that mean much to us: birthdays, anniversaries, life moments, and achievements. These can be personal to us, common to our family and friends, or be national. But we might go further and celebrate the longest and shortest days, harvest time and other events of the natural year. These would be very different according to where we live on the Earth's surface but will always transcend the personal at the same time as they influence it.

The festive cycle

In Europe we have become accustomed to the year having four seasons, with roughly equal weight, but elsewhere it is not so. Consider the polar regions where the year is more like a long *day*, or equatorial regions where without a calendar the *year* would be scarcely noticeable. Different plants have their own cycle too. Hazel catkins and snowdrops may flower together but their fruiting or seed maturation times are months apart and the whole cycle of many other plants has come to fruition in between. For earthly *life* there are really three seasons: *preparing*, *growing* and *ripening* (or *dying*) and *ingathering*. It is with Earth's daylight that we experience four seasons—equinoxes and solstices—in the festival year, in the Earth's *breath* or soul. However, for our purposes this fourfoldness will be put to the background; it is with the threefoldness that we can discover a free approach to festival celebration. Why?

We take our starting point from what we shall (after St Paul) call the 'Second Creation', which began, according to recent researches,[1] on 3 April AD 33 with the crucifixion of Jesus under the Romans. In his letter to the church in Corinth St Paul writes (2 Cor. 5:17), 'if anyone is in Christ he is in a new creation', Christ being the 'new Adam', the beginning of a new epoch in human evolution. For the purposes of this book, I would characterize 'in Christ' as placing oneself 'in' the creative dynamic of the festival-year. The key events and years preceding and following that day of resurrection make a chain that leads through the qualities of the three fundamental seasons: preparation, growth and death and ingathering or: *Christmas*, *Easter* and *Whitsun*.

Now, it is the characteristic of any living thing that each of its parts is an image or representative of the whole, and this is what we find in the year. The three groups of festivals each have three festivals within them and these three parts have qualities relating them to the three main groups. So Advent, Christmas and Epiphany taken all together stand as a beginning, like Advent; yet Christmas already carries the touch of Easter—a birth or rebirth, and Epiphany carries one of Whitsun—a going out into the world. For simplicity we can say for now that the three components are past, present and future.

Taking these three *natural* seasons we group the Christian festivals as follows:

Preparation: Advent, *Christmas*, Epiphany and Candlemas—PAST
Growth and Death: Lent, *Easter*, Ascension—PRESENT
Ingathering: *Whitsun*—FUTURE.

Growing out of Whitsun are festivals which are the real human response to what a high being from beyond this world, whose humanity far exceeded anyone else's, has done. We look upon Christ as the bearer of the creative Word who has contracted from the cosmic dimensions of Creator to become united with his Creature, the pure earthly being Jesus, who referred to himself as 'Son of Man'. The truth about this union is still being sought: it is partly to be found in the cycle of the year. The festivals from Advent to Whitsun are given to us through the deeds of this being; from Whitsun through to Advent are the festivals that *we ourselves have to initiate*: Midsummer (St John's Tide), Lammas, Michaelmas, All Saints' and All Souls' Days. That is our own harvest, our own future, which then enables us to bring the initiative of partnership into creating the cycle of the year in the festival form. It is also our path towards becoming Son of Man ourselves, something that this book tries to illustrate. I hope you will find, as you work through the chapters, that, although the above is an outright Christian statement, its fruits can be harvested by all of us, regardless of belief.

This cycle of the seasonal processes in the conception, growth-and-death and harvest of Christ-Jesus is what he has bequeathed us to be faithfully or 'religiously' repeated. It thereby becomes *religion*, one that acts within us as a ferment of its own creative dynamic.

Earth festivals and religion

The traditional seasonal festivals of ancient times, with their religious aspects of creativity, fertility, fruitfulness and death, had much in common over the Earth, yet emphasis was different according to the local nature of the year and its crops. Vital to these celebrations was the expression of the relationship to the powers working in the events or occasions they celebrated, whether nature powers or the great powers that created and ordered the world and worked for its fruitfulness and that of each human life upon it. The gods, the powers of the elements, the spirits of the creatures, all had to be met in festivals, also the genii of human tribes and individuals.

These ancient motifs of Nature and Spirit in celebrating the year have come over into many of our modern festivities. In Judaism a New Year or a Harvest festival has its place in the cycle of the year as it celebrates events in the historical biography of the nation, notably Passover, the escape from bondage in Egypt. In Europe, where Celtic religions were deeply established, the Christian church had to absorb and reclothe them in its own colours rather than try to eliminate them, and local struggles between the church and the 'old religion' went on for a very long time—indeed continues today, and I hope you will be able to find some kind of higher synthesis of them here. Thus the forerunner of Candlemas, a major Celtic festival called Imbolc, became a commemoration of the presentation of Jesus in the temple and the purification of the Virgin on that day (2 February, see Luke 2:22–3) replacing the festival of the light goddess Brigid (1 February). The leitmotif was the marking of the events of the life of Jesus Christ as the church saw them, using pre-Christian festivals as a platform on which they could be celebrated. Indeed the timing of the events of the life of Jesus fitted almost perfectly into the existing festivals. They were supported by nature and the First Creation, that is, that which set moving the evolution of mankind on the Earth.

What we wish to do here is the converse: to show, and practise, that the events of the life of Jesus Christ can be a platform for the right celebration of *nature*, to make a *Second* Creation. What are the criteria for the steps that will take us forwards from here to a free forming of effective festivals?

Gaia and ecology: a moral attitude to nature

The Earth is no longer young, developing and everlasting. She demonstrably has natural limits. She has been created as the arena on which human life and evolution could unfold; she is there for us to complete our lives' journeys and encounters with one another. But she is showing that she needs nurture if she is to continue providing children with early memories of her beauty, providing folk with sustenance.

While early festivals were to give to nature and her divinities the recognition and the life substance of human beings as a thanksgiving, to appease and sustain her, this was still from man as a *nature* being. Gradually, however, humanity has emancipated itself considerably from nature; and this is the current and essential step for our longer-term evolution towards autonomy, as free individualities in the world of all beings. We are no longer the child of an all-nurturing Mother. We have become teenagers, looking for our own way in life, still using parental resources—sometimes extravagantly—and causing many parental headaches. We have to move on now to become able to *sustain* the Earth herself.

Of a plant that has blossomed and set seed we may say that the powers of the sky—Sun, Moon, stars and climate—have raised it up from the Earth, developed it and warmed it to ripeness. Now, to reproduce it, the Earth must absorb it into herself and imbue it with *her* own qualities, namely her image of what that plant was and should be again. We are saying here that we ourselves must play the role of sky by raising nature up, and then give her seed back to her to see what she makes of it. This is, in a sense, a holy deed for the future of mankind on Earth.

So we are not wanting to talk about Christian festivals as they have been traditionally celebrated but are looking for ways in which each of us can authentically celebrate the year in its parts to carry it rightly through creativity and fertility towards fruitfulness, death and resurrection.

The cycle of the year here presented is a matrix for developing this creativity in such a way that, like any good seed, it produces a surplus. Renewal of the festive year is a feeding of the Earth and ourselves with this surplus. 'Ecological' (Gk *oikos* = house, 'eco') should mean a Second Creation, rebuilding the *house* of Earth. This is not simply a dogmatic prerequisite for utilizing this book; I do not mean that you need to believe this before using the book. I just want to invite you to come with me on this journey of observation, research and experimentation to see what harvest it brings.

Morality

The word moral has been cheapened by 'moralizing'—one person telling another what they ought to do. But our modern morality can have a much more powerful meaning. Terrible acts against human dignity beginning in the last century were the shadow thrown by the very positive ability to feel one's way into the soul and feeling of another person—just that ability that was completely absent in the perpetrators of brutality. The word *empathy* was born. We no longer need rely on outer codes of behaviour when we can perceive what another person must be feeling. Actions that take full account of these perceptions are 'moral' ones, and if we use this faculty of empathy towards nature we can develop a moral relationship to her by helping her to grow beyond herself. My hope is that in developing our festivals along the lines sketched out here we shall have a real experience that this form of morality does actually imbue life with a totally new quality. This permeates nature through our use of her gifts in each festival with a quality which comes to her from 'without', out of the realm of the future, through the human being. Nature in her totality is then given a seed that *grows* with each celebrated cycle of the year, free from the ageing and dying elements within her. Can we begin to see that the force of resurrection released into the world at the first Easter endows mankind with this power to re-enliven something in nature which will carry her over into a still to be imagined new stage of evolution? Human beings exert their privilege and responsibility in a second Creation.

It is this morality—or new creation—that is sown in the resurrection and given wings at Whitsun, when the Spirit enters all, of whatever race and nation . . . and religion.

The inspiration for this is contained in the books and lectures of Rudolf Steiner. He contributed total innovation in many spheres of life, such as education, medicine, agriculture, economics, science, religion, art and architecture. He gave valuable guidance in all aspects of personal spiritual development and meditation, including insights for evaluating and sometimes embracing practices of other disciplines.

These insights are relevant to this day. Rudolf Steiner does truly stand as the teacher of the whole epoch.

1
SOME BASICS

The chapters

We shall take a fresh look at the *style* of each festival. We shall see, for example, that snow is not an essential aspect of Christmas but a seasonal, *natural* accoutrement in some parts of the globe. What is important is the cold. The coldness into which the Child is born is of the human heart, depicted outwardly by winter and snow. In Europe, generally speaking, nature provides parables for the festivals; in the other parts of the world this is not immediately evident and something new needs to be discovered, e.g. how to portray cold in a hot climate.

Each chapter follows a common pattern, describing the motif of the festival—what it is primarily about—within our own local natural surroundings. We shall use it as a kind of window through which to search nature, to select what can be taken to illustrate and enhance it, to interpret it for daily awareness. Any biblical background is then referenced and led over into meditation and prayer. By meditation we mean to look at something quietly until its inner nature dawns upon our mind. The first step is to clear away preconceptions, describe the content objectively, *ponder* it, i.e. feel its weight, its relationship to what is earthly, and then *consider* it, i.e. feel its connection to the stars (*cum sideribus*, Lat. with the stars), to the widest perspective, to what is long-lasting or of eternal worth.

By contemplating a mere detail, like where the right place for a candle might be, or something major that may take years to be answered, like what is the right colour background, we open up an inner activity and attitude, repeatedly cultivated in order to establish a real, personal, but also objective and fully fruitful aesthetic judgement. Whether we live in the Northern or Southern Hemisphere, our mind will sooner or later light up with a picture of what to do to create our festival. We shall also feel more confident, having a maturer judgement after repeating the process the following year. (Yes, this kind of 'learning' develops in a time scale of *years*—not surprisingly considering the topic!)

A word about meditation and prayer

Meditation is traditionally used in English to mean a deeper kind of musing. It is used like this to begin with, to help us to a broader perspective and deeper grasp of what the festival is. Later it is deepened further still. It is also used in anthroposophy, the name for the body of work achieved by Rudolf Steiner referred to in Chapter 1. It means being conscious of our humanity in its widest, spiritual sense and purpose. It is a mental exercise that takes a particular thought and attempts to strengthen it and connect it with all our other thoughts. Steiner's basic books outline various approaches to this. The following are the main ones:

Theosophy:[2] having faith in one's own faculty of reasoning to study safely the works of spiritual science (anthroposophy);
Knowledge of the Higher Worlds:[3] general guidance in spiritual exercises and encountering their results;
The Stages of Higher Knowledge:[4] developing further some aspects of the previous work;
Occult Science: An Outline:[5] Chapter 10 gives an example of how a meditation is built up and carried out.

We achieve thereby a greater picture, whose components fit harmoniously together. It is a *will* exercise as well as being a mental one, because of the concentration needed.

The examples offered in each chapter are given to provide a broader perspective to the basic motif and to help deepen our experience of it over time. It is recommended that before starting any meditative work, the advice given by Rudolf Steiner be followed. To give a firm basis for a meditative practice, there are some basic exercises to help safeguard the student from any negative side effects that poor functioning might allow in and to help bring out the best from the effort made. They involve exercises that help cultivate good habits like disciplined timing, concentration, selflessness and openness. Once they are established, one may take up a particular text, verse or image recommended for the purpose (by a suitable teacher) for meditation proper. One does not need a personal teacher if one has access to Rudolf Steiner's works on the subject because they are bound to be more suitable. What is often valuable, however, is to have someone able to guide the way through these works. The material given here in the 'meditation' section of each chapter is recommended for quiet contemplation and pondering. It is not intended to be taken up as mantric material or replace the content one might already be working with but rather as an extension of it in which that same depth of soul is applied. They will prepare us inwardly to notice the moments in which something lights up as a new, creative idea.

Prayer is another way of deepening our grasp of the festival. Although prayer built up on clear, well-integrated thoughts certainly works well, this is not essential. Here it is the *intention* that is all-important. We can pray about things we do not understand—while furthering that understanding through contemplation and meditation. To turn an inner activity of thought and feeling into prayer we must address it to a higher being and we must *will* that it be loosed from us upon its way towards this being, like rising incense. May it be used for good somewhere, whether in the world or within the being of the one praying. The suggestions to be given for prayer indicate inner moods, outer areas needing change, or people for whom prayer would be valuable.

In prayer and meditation, *time* is measured not only in minutes but in *attitude*. With the right attitude, much can be achieved in but a few moments.

With patience you are sure to discover through prayer and meditation and the contemplation of nature that your festivals gradually become more alive. Year by year you will grow with them, giving and receiving, leading and imitating, being challenged and finding the unexpected joy and peace out of which are born the unexpected enthusiasm, vision and the blessings of your own future!

To Christians on the southern side of the world

Our attitude to nature leads on to the conviction that there is no cause to change the timing of festivals in other parts of the world to fit them to the same *season* of the year in which they were established in Europe. This misses the wholeness of the Earth and its sleeping-waking mantle of humanity. Further aspects of this are to be found in the appropriate chapters, which, it is hoped, will also be helpful to those whose Christmas candles might be sagging during the heat of midsummer in a southern continent.

We have seen already that the power that is to flow into nature through our efforts in the ways indicated is 'trinitarian', the trinity of preparation, growing/dying and ingathering, or Christmas, Easter and Whitsun—as outlined in the previous chapter. Nature will gradually be inwardly changed. The existing four-seasons year of equinox-solstice will gradually become a three-seasons year. It once was so in for example ancient Egypt (flooding, sowing and harvesting); but now it will be born out of the spirit rather than nature. There will be: December–February, 'Christmas'; March–May, 'Easter'; and June–October, 'Whitsun'. Then in November we pause, re-establishing our links with those who have passed beyond the threshold of death and play their part in world affairs from the other side. The question of reversing the festivals in the Southern Hemisphere will thus steadily diminish in relevance, as long as the work here described is joyfully fulfilled; for this work will truly transform the Earth.

2
ADVENT

Motif

Our mood changes the moment we realize a visitor is on the way. This is 'Advent', meaning 'he is coming', and it focuses our attention on preparation. Who is he? Why is he coming? What shall we do for him, with him?

Each group of festivals begins with this character of questioning: Christmas with its preparation during Advent, Easter with the self-examination of Lent, and Whitsun with the renewing of a whole community.

The essence of Advent is to come to terms with the past in order to prepare for the future. This has three aspects. First we have to do with the historic coming into the world of the 'Light of the World', the creative Sun-power which, as we shall see, transforms darkness and makes for colour in life. As creator of the world he enters his creation as *creature* to transform the creature into a *creator.*

Secondly, Advent is announced by the two men seen standing by the disciples saying, 'He will *come again* in the same way that you saw him go' (Acts 1:11). This and other biblical texts point to a mystery of Christianity full of questions. Was the Incarnation an isolated event, at the end of which Christ 'ascended into heaven' and disappeared? Does he reincarnate as some proclaim? Or is there a third possibility, which we may try to grasp step by step and which is the key idea behind this? Finally, we can try to gather up the past year to help us to a fresh start for the one ahead.

Nature

Images taken from nature can help us grasp spiritual realities and we can start with an example from the first chapter of the Acts of the Apostles (vv. 9–10): 'A cloud took him out of their sight; he will come again in the same way that you saw him go.' We observe clouds either for their beauty or to forecast the weather and we know that they are of all shapes and sizes. There is, however, a kind of archetypal cloud that is at the centre of all the variations of cloud formation and stands out clearly from the rest. This is called the *cumulus* cloud because it *piles up* (or ac*cumulates*). A small cloud forms, then grows little by little as water vapour rises up from the ground and is absorbed, making the cloud grow into something resembling a loose cauliflower. In the right conditions it can become very large indeed and can generate a kind of thin veil draped gracefully over the summit like a delicate petal, sometimes two, three or more lie one over the other—a rare and beautiful sight! After this stage has been reached there may be hail and thunder. The petal formation may then lift off to become *cirrus* clouds, 'mare's tails' that float high in the air (cirrus means curl); and the lower sections of the cloud may become heavy and flat and sink down as *stratus*. These three forms are the three basic ones. The central one, cumulus, actually depicts for us the realm of life. It passes through the same growth process as the plant; it grows upwards, bears a blossom, gives forth seed (hail or rain) and dies away. The two men who speak the words quoted above are saying in effect that Christ will return in the realm of Life—both in human biography and in the biosphere of the Earth, all those areas that nowadays concern us because we have realized that it is this realm that bears us in our life. Perhaps Christ bears both.

However, we can do more than study the way that clouds grow and move in this season because, typically, December weather is dreary and seldom shows this cloud growth. The dullness, however, can be broken by amazing displays of brightness during the day and of colour towards evening. The sky colour displays orange and dark purple: orange light illuminates the clouds on one side and casts purple shadows on the other.* The orange is 'real' because it is brought about by the atmosphere darkening the whiteness of the sun to orange, whereas the purple is a real picture, caused by the grey of the cloud taking on the colour complementary to the orange by a 'trick of the light'. These are two quite different processes that nature gives us here and they remind us that we live in worlds of varying degrees of 'reality'.

Many of us are familiar with coloured 'after-images'. They involve our own inner constitution of the living processes (glandular, organic ones, etc. and their counterparts imperceptible to physical means) as well as our

*'Purple' is used here as it is closer to the actual experience we have in looking. Strictly speaking of course the colour that is complementary to orange is blue. The sky is not *in* a science laboratory; it is one.

physical sense perception. What we are looking at now is a complex phenomenon, as though we were seeing nature's own after-image (called 'simultaneous contrast') where the complementary colour 'appears' in an otherwise colourless space.

Something similar happens within the soul: we have our experiences and try to assimilate them but they leave a shadow—because we have not yet fully grasped them. We are reminded that all the thoughts and feelings we have are but an approximation of the total reality, an inner light which is 'darkened' by the atmosphere of life's details. There is always something left over, sometimes seen by others, sometimes by no one. However, if we inwardly watch, the complement appears gradually in the soul, a real picture that is a soul reality of what is still 'coming' towards us in terms of destiny. This is a very subtle experience that is usually covered by the flavour of modern life, but when we can perceive it we realize it is telling us something of what will happen in our life to enable us to make the action or experience whole, complete, within the perspective of the whole of life in space and time. In inner silence we notice our potential to grow. It is this that makes it like an after-image: the force of 'life' draws it from the wholeness of the spirit into that shadow in our own world cast by our inadequacy. It is a picture of our future destiny. We awaken on a higher level.

Biblical context

The reference in Acts 1 has already been mentioned. Other images that fill out the qualities of Advent are:

1. Matthew 25:1–13, describes maidens called to attend the bridegroom, five wise enough to bring spare lamp oil, five foolish. When the bridegroom finally arrives, the foolish ones are absent buying more oil but are shut out by the bridegroom who says, 'I know you not.' What is lamp oil within our human soul? Preparedness, faithfulness, watchfulness, devotion?
2. Luke 21 describes images of the world chaos and turmoil that accompanies this cosmic-terrestrial process called the coming of the Son of Man. 'Son of Man' is the biblical phrase for the part of the inner human being that is currently being evolved. This meant one thing in ancient Egypt and means something different now. At the time of Christ it referred to the human 'I' that Christ

was bearing in himself to convey to mankind. That is why it is so confusing: it sometimes refers to himself, at others to those generally in active inner development. This challenging glimpse into the surge of spirit behind world events can help us see how we can be active and thereby gives us courage.

3. In the Old Testament, stories of the conception in unlikely situations occur with Isaac (Gen. 18:9), Samuel (Sam. 1:17), Samson (Judg. 13:3), and in the New Testament, John the Baptist (Luke 1:15). They tell of some of the necessary preparations, are forerunners of the birth of Jesus, and their stories can inspire our soul's journey towards the 'birth' we try to achieve within us at Christmas.

Meditative pictures

1. Think of an inner Sun as well as the outer one. Not only does the Sun's light and warmth give us *life* but the warmth of the Sun *Spirit* once gave birth to the Earth itself and modified it with its light. But *creative* light can become *inspiring* light. Try to feel: as this Sun-power penetrates us, the love expressed in the process of creation takes root in us and becomes love for our neighbour, which is a human expression of the morality discussed already in Chapter 1. This is the essence of 'cosmic' Christianity because it relates to a Christianity that looks upon Jesus Christ not only as Man, a *human* being, but a divine one too, related spiritually to the physical Sun. In biblical terms, the Son of God, the divine part, becomes Son of Man, the human part, whether in Jesus or in us.
2. The second aspect of Advent is the coming into our world of the same being in a different form and in a different realm at a different time: here and now. He enters the realm of biography and destiny where something new is needed, i.e. the realm of *life* in its broadest sense. Where can this beginning of a *new creation* happen except within the human heart and within relationships between people? It will pass us by if we are not ready; life will in that eventuality not just stagnate but worsen, like a growing plant we did not water at the right time, so forfeiting its harvest. So an activity shared, whether creatively connected with the approach

to Christmas or in study, as long as the quality of relationship is nurtured, helps this 'second coming' recur annually as part of the year's rhythm, like a pulse of spiritual lifeblood, as *personal* Christianity. As this develops we would say that everyone grows beyond themselves by opening to that which is higher and greater, or: the Son of God helps us give birth to the Son of Man within. (The *active* principle is called 'Son', the *embracing* one is the divine female part of our own soul.) The idea here is that within human destinies something as important as the creation of the world can come about.

3. The scientific mind may meditate here on the 'open places' in modern ideas, where we are at a frontier of knowledge. Here are some examples. What is the true nature of light? What happened before the big bang? What is 'between' the atomic particles—or the galaxies? Or we may ponder on the nature of God and whether our experience of the world is real. What has each of the great religions to say about these things and where in it all are we finding our own orientation? Questions such as these are good to ponder during Advent, for when pondering an earnest question in a spiritual context, answers (often in the form of further questions) are sure to come—if we are patient and watchful—as an 'after-image'.
4. There is a deeper mystery to Advent, however. It can really be a time of year when we inwardly prepare not just to re-enact an important part of history but to pay some attention to spiritual development, remembering that it can only be fruitful if tempered by perseverance and humility. World affairs are shaken open for change by spiritual powers in response to human activity of this kind. Look outwards into world events. How far do the effects of nations upon one another depend upon the activities of the individuals within them, or influences from outside? How far are they brought about by world evolution, for example in genetic research or in ideas about euthanasia where the views and practices of one country have a marked effect on others, for better or worse? Or what are the human consequences of natural catastrophes? We have referred to the Divine Creator. Now we open up another dimension of the spiritual world, the heavenly hierarchies. Rudolf Steiner has given an extremely comprehensive view of this realm, enhancing greatly the traditional

theologies that go back to Dionysius the Areopagite and the Apostle Paul himself—a renewal of cabbalistic and other ancient traditions. For now, we are looking at those standing just above Man in evolution. Depending on the answers to the above questions, we can gain an impression of the involvement in earthly affairs of three different ranks of this neighbouring hierarchy. Where *individuals* are concerned, we may see the working of *Angels*; where whole nations are engaged, *Archangels*; with world evolution, *Archai* or Spirits of the Age (*Zeitgeist*). With catastrophes, we see the influence of spiritual beings of higher rank still. This is all a suitable subject for contemplation during Advent because of Christ's words to Nathanael, 'you will see heaven opened and the Angels of God ascending and descending upon the Son of Man' (John 1:51). We develop this 'Son of Man' within us according to the way we cope with these world events, for that is how we evolve as personalities, grow in stature, giving birth to our own future self.

We are not attempting here anything more than to awaken a feeling for this wider dimension. For further research, see *Spiritual Beings in the Heavenly Bodies and the Kingdoms of Nature*,[6] Rudolf Steiner Press.

Prayer

Advent prayers are about making a new start. We can ask for guidance for individuals on their life-path, that their path be towards wisdom and light. Likewise the destinies of nations—are they moving towards the quality of light and love for which this festival exists, that ideal of humanity that is so obviously at stake in strife between nations, races or individuals? We can pray that what unites become stronger than what divides and this can be extended to humanity as a whole. Do our values stand up to the test of kneeling before a sleeping newborn infant? Are we as nations working to harmonize our national gifts for a better symphony?

If we know the Lord's Prayer, introduced in Matthew 6 and Luke 11, we may think of the line about the Kingdom, that it may come—that an order of life may be established on Earth that is in harmony with the wholeness of the universe. That the *divine* will be done (the next line) need not be an abdication of our own free initiative. It does not mean that we just want to obey someone else to spare ourselves the trials of self-determination. It means that our own will may grow in harmony with the universe and that our own motives may be inspired by a caring for the wholeness of humanity and her evolution. These are helpful attitudes when we are preparing for the future that is coming towards us—all of us!

Contemplation of nature in northern and southern continents

Some riddles about their polarity and how together they make a whole

Try to take what comes here as a kind of real myth, not meant as allegory but as one *reality* lying *behind* another. Its needs to be read with imagination, withholding mental analysis until the picture is complete and has yielded up its mood.

When we are awake, we stand separate from other kingdoms of creation in that our self-consciousness lives within us on the same level as our sense perception. We know who we are. In animals, this spirit element of consciousness is only there on a dream level, as one can often see, working through their instincts. When we sleep, however, we have no self-consciousness and no sensation; our spirit and soul are, so to speak, 'outside' our body, no longer connected to the sense world, whilst our inner, organic processes are able to work away undisturbed by the demands of the soul.

Let us now try to draw a parallel between this and the Earth. We can say that in summer, when everything is at its fullest extent of growth and splendour, the Earth is asleep—its soul is outside and its consciousness is in the periphery. It is 'unfolded'. In winter, however, the landscapes, light and the starry sky exhibit a distinct clarity, a wakefulness. In the Northern Hemisphere, then, during winter, nature is drawn into the Earth, is infolded, is awake. Although the life cycles of plants begin at various points in the year, we can imaginatively say that in winter seeds are in general in the phase *before* germination, as though waiting in the ground to know what they are to become. Rudolf Steiner was able to describe[7] how the elementary spirits of moist air and light unite themselves with the form of the plant as they stretch out its shoots and leaves and organize its chemistry of photosynthesis and deposition of carbon compounds to give it its 'fibre'. They then keep their impressions of this form as it is released into spirit as the body of the plant decays, then give them over to the earth spirits waiting below, looking after the ripened, fallen seeds. (At germination, this 'dreamed' form unites with the seed, informing its growth patterns.)

Let us just look for a moment at our experiences of midsummer and midwinter at both midday and midnight.

At midnight in December the stars are near, but they are 'up above'. There is a distance between us but it is bridged by a kind of silent communication. At midsummer, the stars are still up above but in a way that our soul can touch them. The bridge between us is our own soul, not any kind of thought or feeling.

At midday in December the sun is up above us but not so high—our soul is big enough to embrace it. But in midwinter the sun is low and our soul safely within us, as a force that holds us safely within the vast space of the world.

In a lecture on midsummer,[8] Rudolf Steiner helps us imagine the Earth below its surface, where, in the darkness, forces gather in blue crystalline forms. I find it not so difficult to imagine, as it creates a good balance to the heat and light up above. It is as though this force is holding everything in clarity so that the Earth's forces will not dissipate in the adventures of summer. As summer progresses, a kind of silvery ray shines upwards and gradually—in the summery atmosphere—turns to gold. This helps give a moral challenge to our conscience to try during that summer period to bring our own life into the same kind of clarity so that it can ray out silvery and give gold to the world.

I was able to experience having my shadow between my feet in the heart of Australia on 21 December. I would therefore say the above holds good during summer there too.

In midwinter, however—and it is asserted that this only goes for the *Northern* Hemisphere—the Earth below its surface is receptive to the light that rays down from the stars. The movement is downwards, not upwards and outwards. Here a kind of self-consciousness takes place, rather as in our own mind we derive self-consciousness from the things of the world that comes towards us. The Earth becomes self-conscious at midwinter as though it were a kind of head in the cosmos. So in June, our northern awareness has been in harmony with that of the Earth since midwinter, flowing *outwards* from a self-conscious centre into an all-pervading soul-universe. But in the *Southern* Hemisphere, the midwinter human soul-wakefulness is not accompanied by that of the Earth itself, as in the north, so the path to midsummer in the

Southern Hemisphere is a different one. This may take some years, or decades, for us to experience and understand properly. Suffice it to say, for the sake of this chapter, that this asymmetry in the polarity of north and south suggests that it would not be a good thing to change festivals in the south to be in the season in which they happen in the north. For the festivals are not seasons; and where the season is different in a particular month that is a stimulus for us to ask what the Earth really then needs from that festival at that time. Certainly they need to be different, as we try to show, but reversal divides the Earth just when we are trying to help her evolve as a single entity.

One way of working into this is to try living with the verses of Rudolf Steiner's *Calendar of the Soul*—one for each week.[9] They typically find a motif from European nature and develop out of it a soul mood. But in this calendar one often finds that the mirror image verse has a clear metamorphosis of the one for that week. This working with two opposite verses at the same time helps us contain the hemisphere dichotomy within our one soul.

Creating your festival

An inner clearing of the soul goes hand-in-hand with an outer clearing of the house and of one's workload. It is good to round off unfinished jobs and correspondence. This frees the soul and she can gaze more freely into nature, remembering that her gaze is searching nature for what can serve the festive celebration. In the north this might be the evergreens and crystals, or resinous woods that make the fire crackle. But in the south it might mean the newly opened blossoms, a butterfly's wing or some token from the vibrant life of bird and insect, or some seed-head heavily pregnant in anticipation of the new life to come.

We are waiting for a birth, so we prepare a place, ideally in the heart of the living space at home, where this birth will be depicted on Christmas morning. But we do not wait till Christmas Eve for that. We do it the night before Advent Sunday so that we approach and enter that space through time, through a whole month. This may be done in various ways, marking the journey day by day and week by week. To get the number of days correct we must bear in mind that Advent begins on the fourth Sunday before Christmas, so may vary in length between 22 and 28 days. Beware of some Advent artefacts that for commercial reasons run from 1 December. The Sunday start is important because Sunday is the first day of the week, an octave of both the first day of the first creation represented in the tradition of Genesis and the 'second creation' at Easter.

An important feature is the portrayal of a child born into a family. We must not forget the importance of Joseph: it is after all *his* genealogy that is given in the Gospels. He can father the Son of God because of his righteousness (his spiritual uprightness) and thus enable the conceiving divine spirit (Holy Spirit) to work its work through him, instead of it being his own earthly private personality that conceives. The conception is virginal in being free from earthly desire ('knowing').

To convey this mood of revisiting the past and tracing it to the present, a deep blue is a favourable background, whilst red, green and gold are the colours that best represent the human, the earthly and the heavenly respectively. To furnish a blue backdrop to the birth-path with silver Moon, golden Sun and stars lifts the soul to the place where the inner light originates, which is to give us the awareness of our equality with all other human beings before this child. The Advent journey is thus a cosmic one, lasting a 'cosmic' month, from Advent Sunday to Christmas Eve. The donkey ride to Bethlehem on the other hand shows an earthly journey, which would have been considerably shorter!

Then evening comes. The last ceremonies are celebrated and quiet falls. If we have children at home we might rush into to feverish activity as soon as they are in bed to make the transition to Christmas. This feels all right if we have managed to fulfil the inner side of the festival along the way and have our soul a tiny bit peaceful and stable, but even then it is of great importance to meet ourselves—and those with whom we live, perhaps also those with whom we worship, in a silent space before sleep.

If we choose to attend a midnight vigil or a midnight communion service then we may try to experience what it is like being religiously awake at a time that is usually that of slumber.

Summary

Advent is a festival period for preparing Christmas. It is a remembering of a tradition based on a past event. It is also a looking ahead to a personal step in a development that can be achieved for the first time now, *in our age,* because of the co-called Second Coming. We develop by the way we meet what comes to us from outside with what we create from within: through the individual light, warmth and vision kindled spiritually that focuses ahead to Christmas.

3
CHRISTMAS

25 December to 6 January

Motif

We have all once been born. That is the essential unifying theme of Christmas and Christianity. Its paradox is its power to unite mankind by bringing to birth the true individuality of each one. It is undeniably rooted in just *one* religion yet different religions may also find meaning in its essential humanity. The basis of Christmas is to *cross thresholds* between peoples.

Nature

In the autumn, heavy seeds of trees fell to the earth. They made for nature's future. Now, ideally and perhaps imaginatively, something else falls to the earth on Christmas Eve. We hold our breath as the gentle flakes of snow drift softly earthwards. Gradually a carpet of whiteness builds up, thicker and thicker as silent moments go by, giving the night a deeper meaning. This is the night of birth, not nature-birth but spirit-birth, the coming to Earth of all souls who will be born during the coming year. This is an imagination: it may also be real. In the morning, all is bright and sparkling: we are inwardly refreshed by the vision and its beauty and step out into Christmas new-born for the future, for humanity will also be reborn through those souls due soon to arrive.

Even if there is no snow, the souls still come! And we can still imagine their soft descent and make ready for them as best we can.

Biblical context

The basic text for Christmas is the Gospel of St Luke. The conception is heralded by a divine messenger, and the name is given beforehand. The divine fatherhood is emphasized, yet the ancestry of an *earthly* father is described: 'son of Joseph, of Heli, of Matthat, of . . . of God' (Luke 3:23–38). There is a heavenly Father (the Holy Spirit!) and an earthly father (Joseph), descended 'genetically', however, from God the Father.

In the conception of an earthly child, there is a lot of 'personality' involved, but if the conception were to be 'immaculate', i.e. without the desire to take, but to give, then the earthly father can be the husbandman of the Spirit of all humanity. This child is laid in a manger (Luke 2:7), is taken into Simeon's arms (Luke 2:28), his mother carries his progress in her heart (Luke 2:51). We gather a source of peace of the inward-drawing kind. This child does not have any false view of us, nor even seems he to have any reaction to us whatever; he only acts, in extreme peace, in glowing elemental dearness and it is *we* who react. We change before him. He is lying down, carried by the Earth, or cradle, or human arms; we react by growing bigger in our hearts. Much can fall away that hinders others seeing us as we would like them to, that hinders them reaching us.

But what of the other side, the world? How do we renew a relationship to that? For this we need the other basic text, the Gospel of St Matthew. The theme is different: the threat of Herod, the powers that take away all peace, put violence into the world and fear in the heart. How much fear is dispensed in our time in even well-meaning ways: risk assessment, insurance, fear of infection, and so on. Herod wanted to hold on to power and spread fear to do so. And it is kings, not shepherds, who visit this child, not representatives of the ordinary individual but of world destiny. And these great guides of humanity acknowledge him as above them: they grow smaller, they kneel, they reveal that part of us which can serve the world, put our gifts to work for the world, without thought of personal aggrandisement. Humble, gracious majesty. This child knows where to send us in the world that the gifts of the first one, the gifts of the heart, be applied in the way only we as individuals can apply them, giving the world our own unique, divinely bestowed gifts..

The child described by Luke has his birthday dated by Ormond Edwards[10] as on 25 December and that described by Matthew on 6 January. However, *that* 6 January is at the *beginning* of the year 1 and that 25 December is at the end. From this point of view the sovereign child is the first and the child of grace the second: he who becomes 'Jesus of Nazareth'.

But the universal child is born into a *family*. The family mediates between the child and the whole of humanity, so this is the archetype of Christmas: to celebrate the family, focusing inwardly on a new birth (i.e.

the birth of something new) into the family and outwardly to friends, neighbours, community, nation, race, all who live on the Earth now, all who have lived and all who will live in the future. If we can feel this birth we can understand what is meant by 'conceived by the Holy Ghost', as expressed in the Apostles' Creed. Biology to one side, the *spirit* of the child is the universal spirit. And if we can extend our family to include all as 'men of good will', peace will follow. The shepherds were greeted by the heavenly host with the words 'the revelation of God in the highest and peace on Earth to men of good will'. The 'holy family' had little more than ox and ass, but they did possess that which the rest of us may lack: true peace, which they gave out freely. So essentially our Christmas must attempt to find our *true* family and look on its holy child: to wonder together quietly at the coming of light from eternity into time.

Meditative pictures

First, on 25 December , we celebrate the child in his manger, visit him as plain folk with humble hearts, then after twelve days, to 6 January, we visit the other, to be directed into the world to develop a sovereignty over our life task there, albeit in humility! However, *that* 6 January is at the *beginning* of the year 1, and that 25 December is at the end.

In everyday life we respond and react to others, and we notice gradually more and more the longer we live how they react in turn to us. We come to accept the fact that what we perceive of ourselves in their reaction is at variance with our self-evaluation. It is into this quality of the Earth at variance with itself that the festival of Christmas descends. It is not merely a children's festival but one for the whole human being; and yet it searches out (or creates?) the child in us, for in the child the self-evaluation comes entirely from the reactions of others, and the division within the soul does not yet exist. And on the other hand, when we confront a very young child, we meet their assessment of ourselves, which is largely positive, and from this side too the division is minimized. At Christmas it is a heavenly child that confronts mankind, not only positively but with the power to raise the human 'humus' into true humanity. The fundamental characteristic of celebrating Christmas is thus to make a home available for the one who arrived homeless on the Earth.

The Holy Nights are a good time to broaden our knowledge of what is known about the spiritual beings ranking between Man and God. What are they like, what do they do? Or take animals—do we really understand them, care for them? Or do we abuse them and destroy them? Can we learn anything about ourselves from them and thus deepen our feeling for their non-humanness and where it needs to be led in evolution? Can we regain the attitude that primitive peoples had of being in a relationship akin to brother with them? The tradition that animals once spoke and may do so again on Christmas night may help us in this.

Another area to ponder is that of human conception. It is no longer held, as it was until recently, that our personality is genetically determined. What does our own experience tell us? How did we feel 'hereditarily' about our parents? Are we aware how much we stand like the one of them or think like the other until we start to make a conscious effort to be ourself? A deep experience of the mystery of Christmas can certainly contribute to this. Gabriel's speech to Zacharias (Luke 1:13) certainly separates the biological John from the spiritual John: he is certainly to be *born* to Zacharias and Elizabeth but will bear the *spirit* of Elijah. The loss of Christmas might well mean the darkening of our spirit by the weight of hereditary nature, but the right celebration of it can once more convince us that, in the words of St John's Prologue, we are formed 'not of blood, nor of the will of the flesh, nor of the will of the Man, but of God' (John, 1:13).

If we base Christmas upon these thoughts and experiences rather than the traditional and now commercial package, we can celebrate also where it is *not* winter. The hot sun floods us with light from which we might outwardly shy away; yet we can take this light as a symbol for self-assessment regarding our relationships within human life, a kind of conscience of our place in space and time. This will help us with those attitudes we have discussed above. We can then imagine this light concentrated into the great star shining above the head of the kingly Christmas child who brings us grace when we apply ourselves to the world, warming us to make a bridge that all might cross between the divisions of race, creed and attitudes within ourselves and those between us and others.

Prayer

The lighting of a Christmas tree can be an important way of extending our hearts to those who are not with us at this festival, whether through distance, suffering or through the outer separation of death—those who 'belong' to us or whom we wish could belong. Visitors during the Holy Nights may also be glad to be part of such a ceremony. Their experience of it is sure to enhance our own. These days may give us a chance of mending a harmed relationship or breaking the ice for a new one; and such things can also be a content for our prayers at this time, for the unity of mankind ('Our' Father), reconciliation of enemies, families damaged by loss of a son or daughter run away, or even those who have lost themselves and their self-esteem. Especially the two themes—'how am I in myself?', 'how am I in the world?'—are appropriate ones for pondering and prayer. 'Love thy neighbour as thyself.' Another theme for prayer can take its start from Psalm 8: man between animal and angel. This is not a higher animal and not a fallen angel but the one who should care for nature and decide to think as an angel. Yet another is the mystery of human life and how this may give us responsibilities for developing it.

Contemplation of nature—in northern and southern continents

Above all, we feel as we study the Gospel texts year after year that they contain mysteries which have not yet fully come to light. There is no mention of cold winter in these narratives. If we live in Borneo or Brazil we do not have to have snow and freezing shepherds. We can ask therefore, what is special here at this time. There are Australian carols which celebrate the fullness of life in the bush, the world out there in active being, which have been created by finding in nature results of Christmas in the world—active harmony—and portray that aspect as well as the quiet waiting that precedes newness.

Creating your festival

The Christian festivals are ones which grow down into our lives out of their own nature, their own inherent character, and it is from there that they transform the soil in which they grow—as certain plants can gradually improve earth into humus, which then enhances the quality of growth there. Like the humus, so the human being is enhanced by the appropriate festival.

If during Advent we made an Advent table or corner, we can sense what parts of it can be carried over into those Holy Nights and what needs to be cleared away.

We spoke of Advent as the preparation for this visitor. Now we must 'make' time for him, time to be doing things together which remind us of his arrival: stories, carols, a crib—and presents.

Secondly, we can make the dual nature of Christmas apparent by separating the two stories out more than is usually done. We must keep the Kings out of sight to begin with and give them until 6 January to arrive, by which time the Shepherds have gone and a house stands in place of the manger. If we begin with these we can add what helps our imagination as it grows wider by 'pondering them' in our hearts (Luke 2:51). We might use the red of new life for Mary's robe and the blue of the evening sky for her cloak which hides stars of guiding light in its folds. We might use green for Joseph's tunic, like the 'Green Man' whose one task in life is to give to the Mother of Earth that which lets her bear, and we can clothe him in the brown of the bare earth when she has borne, the brown in which all colours can be found mingled. And he needs a staff, not to lean on but rather to emphasize his inner uprightness—even when his body is beginning to gesture age.

True presents, despite the abundance of the commercial world, are hard to find, unless one has a true interest in the other person, in just that area where we care what we think about each other. The present only works if it is the outer symbol of half a warmth bridge that invites the other to meet it, in order that Christmas grace can bear something new across the chasm of personality to move the relationship onwards. Peace is active, dynamic, and stirs us as it comes to the birth. Peace is the quality of our relationship to everything outside us when it is both humble and sovereign.

If we want a *Christmas* tree it should *be* one, and not be decorated until Christmas Eve, in the evening. We can have an Advent tree already earlier, but then it is a tree of memory of the descent through time from the Tree of Knowledge in Paradise from which Man has been excluded. We may hang an apple there but not light it up or put on it a star or anything else. The Christmas tree must in contrast be able to *radiate* light. Once Christmas has arrived the tree is a good place for some of the gifts—especially some for unexpected guests who surprise us in joy by their coming. Tree gifts can be felt to come from the Christmas Spirit itself, or the tree fairy for children.

But how can we apply all this? One of the wonders of the human mind is its depth. If we look ahead and think about something, we can enter into it much more deeply, even if we do not make real those actual thoughts that we had. So if we spend some time alone, or with someone whose life is close to ours, to look ahead at the coming year month by month for each day of the Twelve Days,* to see what is coming and what we want to bring to it out of the insights Christmas is bringing, we shall find that when the month comes we shall meet it more directly and it will have a more challenging and demanding nature than before. For what we shall then have done is bring the child of grace and blessing within us into dialogue with the one who will meet us in the world, awaiting us in our tasks there, to bring order and sovereignty into what we do. Even if we do not do this fully, some kind of looking ahead is effective, especially on a daily basis. We wake up differently in the morning if we have planned the day beforehand, and so it is with the year.

Likewise, to prepare for the Kings on 6 January, it is important that the accoutrements of Christmas be removed and replaced by symbols suitable for this next festival of Epiphany.

Summary

Christmas celebrates the birth of a child into a special family. A birth unites those who are around it: the birth of Jesus unites humanity—the great family. He is conceived, spiritually, by the spirit of humanity, the Holy Spirit. By celebrating Christmas, whether with or without family, we enact a new birth within us of our spiritual self. That has the power to overcome differences with others and thereby contribute, through true love, to the uniting of mankind.

* Day 1 is 6 p.m. Christmas Eve to 6 p.m. on Christmas Day and corresponds to 22 December to 21 January, approximately, in a qualitative way. A day measured from midnight to midnight corresponds then to a month measured from the first of one month to the first of the next.

4
EPIPHANY

6 January

Motif

Epiphany has two aspects. It originally commemorated the baptism of Jesus in the River Jordan when he was about 30 years old but then came to mark the coming of the Three Magi. Epiphany means a 'shining out upon'—first the star that showed the virtue of the being that was coming to birth (the coming of light), then the dove, the divine spirit of humanity entering evolution in the 'creature' Jesus to make him *Christ*, the anointed one of God (in Hebrew, *Messiah*), expected to be heralded by a star.

Epiphany is thus a festival in which light plays an important part: the gold of the birth star and the white of the spirit-dove.

Nature

Let us look especially now at the play of *light and colour* in nature; different natural features work together to make our world a tableau of colour. Let us distinguish three main realms here: sky, trees and earth. They reveal, as the year unfolds, the light, the dark and the life of colour in the annual cycle of the year.

Try to see in the sky how many shades of blue there are and how the Sun colours the sky and, indeed, itself at sunrise and sunset. We discover the polarity of blue and yellow, the archetypal phenomenon of colour in nature (see the chapter on Michaelmas). How does nature colour itself at these times? What colours and complementary colours appear on the clouds at different times of the day? And if the sky is slightly hazy, what colours appear in their shadows? Usually we take in such perceptions in a dreamy way. Now we can make ourselves conscious of them and awaken to them as though an artist has painted them especially for us.

What colours appear on tree trunks and on the youngest twigs tipped with buds according to their own nature? And how are they affected when all the above colour variants illumine them? Try to distinguish at a distance the purple of a birch bud from that of an alder bud and follow how they change colour during these weeks. Then watch a green morning light or orange afternoon light altering these twig and bud colours or a sunset transfiguring the trunks of mighty trees against an indigo cloud or within a rainbow. Do not these really stand out to us in a special way? The natural world appears now as a weaving of colour, rather than a juxtaposition of 'things'. We gain a more lively relationship to matter. Matter in nature 'shines out', has its *Epiphany*, in such a way as to become the garment for the newly awakened forces unfolding within her.

Now a glimpse at the earth, the soil. We might not be totally aware of it or just know one soil type; but as we travel we may notice different types. We learn to distinguish clayey from loamy or sandy soil, then the colours of the different rocks. Recently ploughed fields give wide stretches of a single colour—and texture. We see long, broken, shiny lines where light is reflected off the fresh-cut surfaces of the furrow. Traversing Britain, we are treated to fairly rapid changes from white to yellow, ochre, orange, red and all shades of brown. Coloured light touches coloured earth. The solid earth and the solid skins of bark and bud are brought into radiance by the colours of the sky quickened by the life of the Sun.

The decision to train such observations to become faithful habits brings about lasting changes in perception, so that it becomes clearer and deeper. The various descriptions presented here can only really come into their own as the fruits of such a decision.

Looking at colour

When one has looked at a colour for a while, it begins to film over and, as one's eye moves slightly, the edges begin to glow. We see the surface more grey but the edges even brighter than the original. The eye projects another colour onto the surface observed. The 'first impression' is modified by one's own physiological activity, just as happens in our soul's experience when we meet somebody. We often soon correct a first impression; but there are times when it does return later on. Often the other responds to this reaction and their own is modified a second time too. Why should not the sense world function in a similar way, i.e. change by being looked at, and change *according to the way* it is looked at? Beauty may *start* in the eye of the beholder but can certainly be engendered in the beheld thereby. Once one is inspired to help the world, one beholds it differently and it responds differently. Surprising and seemingly inexplicable occurrences take place. One can form the idea that not only do other people react positively to us if we shine upon them but that nature does this too. It is easy to say that the world stays the same and merely *looks* different because of our mood; but why should nature in the sense world not react and respond as another person does when 'shone upon'? In this respect Epiphany can be a starting point for something to be developed through the year that will help us anchor our inner festivals into the natural cycle.

Biblical context

The Epiphany season extends from Epiphany day, 6 January, to around Candlemas on 2 February. Two separate events are commemorated on 6 January: the birth of the kingly Messiah and the visit of the Three Magi as described in the second chapter of Matthew; and the baptism of Jesus by John in the Jordan in AD 30 referred to by all four evangelists (see below). Both events are entries into the earthly sphere, the sense world, of a spiritual and supersensible being: first, a great teacher of wisdom, heralded by a star, followed by star-Magi, star-lore initiates; and then 'the Spirit of God in the bodily form of a dove' (Luke 3:22, author's rendering). Finally, after having overshone him for 30 years, the Creator entered and transformed the grown man, Jesus of Nazareth, making him Jesus Christ, the Son of God.

You will note here that the expressions 'Jesus' and 'Christ' are not synonymous. Jesus is the *man* (see Pilate's words, John 19:5) who is anointed ('christ-ened') during the three years between the baptism and the crucifixion, where step by step the human being is purified and prepared for the great task of battling with death.

It was this that was first celebrated as '*Christ*mas', but later the emphasis was changed to the *birth* and moved to its present place in the year, just three days after the shortest day, when the Sun rises victorious over the darkness.

At Epiphany this essence of heaven shines out upon mankind. Modern research using Gospel clues dates the event described in Matthew (star, house, Herod, etc.), while the clues of Luke (Tiberius, shepherds, manger) point to late December of the same year.[11] Without going further into the mystery described little by little in the Gospel, which would go beyond the scope of this book, we can be more true to these inherited texts by separating out the shepherd story from the kingly one rather than sewing them together in the way of our time. By doing this, we can also gain deeper insights into the Incarnation as it unfolds in stages.

A second light is being added to the first, to enhance it with the shining spirit and warmth-substance that is born out of Jesus offering his life, his very being, for the rest of humanity. The direction of this light is out into the world, a warm light, bringing the warmth of dedication to the needs of the world. Having separated out the two aspects of this festival we can now recombine them. We scrutinize ourselves for the child *within* who can be called up into the kingly task which is *out there* for us in the world but which we have not yet discovered or attempted. Then we search out those areas in our life where we are wise rulers already (there are certainly some, even if not noticed!) and let them serve what has newly awakened in us during Christmas. Finally we try to gather the whole into a form where it can be 'baptized'—opened to the heavens to be quickened by that higher power which has well accompanied it from our own birth. It seeks the universal to overcome the personal to bless what we then create as our task for the year. This is reflected in the narrative of Christ's temptation in the soul's wilderness (Matt. 3:16–17; Mark 1:10–11; Luke 3:21–2; John 1:32–4). These are temptations such as the desire for power, depicted by the lofty mountain, the feeling that we can do what we want in life without responsibility, depicted by the pinnacle of the temple, or the sheer force of materialistic possessions, even the thought that we can be truly nourished by them, depicted by the temptation to turn stones into bread. What our life reaps in one year from this effort at selflessness then receives, as a gift from Heaven, a kingly attribute for use in the following year—an attribute that we can give to the world. Thus do the two powers of Christmas and Epiphany, i.e. the humble attitude of devoting ourselves to others and the sense of inner rulership, work alternatingly in time, enhancing one another.

Meditative pictures

1. The house, the star, the aged Joseph, educated and responsible, the maiden mother Mary with the infant upright on her knee, greeting the bowing King (Magus) with hand raised in a regal gesture of grace and blessing. The gold, frankincense and myrrh are placed at her feet one by one. Silence. Who speaks? What is said? What happens afterwards to the gifts? What happens to the Magi as they go home 'by another way'? (Matt. 2:12.)

2. The river—the open sky meeting the hills all around—desert—the disciples of John questioning—John himself watching how Jesus walks, knowing he is the one, and that it is time to fulfil his instructed task—Jesus enters the water—John submerges him—what do they experience? Jesus is lifted up—the spirit of God descends upon him in the bodily form of a dove and remains—he goes into the desert and is tempted. (Matt. 3:16–17; Mark 1:10–11; Luke 3:21–2; John 1:32–4.)
3. As thought and study themes: the birth narratives in Matthew 2 and Luke 2 and the baptism accounts in Matthew, Mark, Luke and John. One can meditate on pictures of the baptism where John the Baptist is shown on one side of the river and facing him on the other are the Archangels Michael, Gabriel and Raphael.
4. Another 'Epiphany' is Arjuna's vision of Krishna in the *Bhagavadgita*—where Krishna the charioteer manifests himself as an aspect of Brahma, a vision described in the most wonderful language, which lifts Arjuna beyond himself. He has a momentary glimpse of the Light of God; and this description can ennoble and elevate, even into our time.

Prayer

The inner gifts of which we are aware in ourselves may very well not match the areas of the world to which we feel called to help. In prayer we can pause in inner stillness, picturing the two—the inner and the outer—and especially against the backgrounds of ordering, maintaining, uplifting, warming, mediating, succouring and blessing, and then use our chosen prayer as a vehicle to let the contemplations rise into the realm where they themselves can be ordered and blest.

Look at the radiant image of the Son of Man and the prayers of the saints at the altar in heaven (Rev. 1, 5 and 8), where what we ourselves pray is received and offered further as 'incense'.

Contemplation of nature—in northern and southern continents

The qualities of nature in other parts of the world are quite different from those of Europe. The light may be much stronger, the trees not bare. Yet our description of this festival has itself not *relied on* any particular natural phenomenon. Admittedly, it is easy to celebrate this cycle of Advent, Christmas and Epiphany in the cold short days of the north; but the *overall* gesture of this cycle is a preparation, reception and bringing into the world of a divine impulse, depicted by the birth of the Messiah. This divine impulse can be felt whenever we are motivated to translate an idea into an ideal, a vision that fires our will to action on the earthly plane. The way we look at nature, attempting to see her as she is and not bound by traditional festival images, forms an approach that is valid worldwide. The same method brings to light different colour moods and colour conversations for each *different* area of the world. Yet the festival motif is the same everywhere. To penetrate a different world of colour with the Epiphany spirit and mood for betterment is truly the final step in the process of transforming our natural Earth through a power of regeneration out of another dimension that may be called 'spirit'. Out of a religious beginning we end with a 'scientific' conclusion: scientific in the sense that it acts in and into the evolutionary processes of the world, perhaps even saving them from disaster! Here, in these other parts of the world, the human soul is working unaided into a nature usually of a different type of vitality and fertility, yet less enhanced by human work than in the Europe of centuries of agricultural cultivation. 'Spirit' is that area of our imagination where our thinking is quickened with ideas that have unfolded through the stimulus of these festivals in their annual round, the path through the year of mankind connecting with birth, death, resurrection and renewal. It can manifest in every practical realm: in agriculture, healing and education. The list is as long as we want to make it.

Creating your festival

This begins in Advent. Already then, we look ahead to Epiphany as the third step following those of the bringing to birth, witnessing birth and living out of birth through the Holy Nights. The tidying, ordering and casting out during Advent helps in evaluating what the year has achieved—for example, progress in changing a particular habit or the healing of a sour relationship. Here both inner and outer things might be thrown away (for example ashtrays or attitudes) and we reassess who we are. This is our material for the coming Epiphany with the question:

What next? The Holy Nights let live in an abbreviated way the 30 years between Jesus' birth and baptism. *If the soul is quiet during these days, to feel that the spiritual world is open, it is ready when heaven closes at the end to open itself to the world.* Our New Year resolutions are, as it were, ordained, anointed, christ-ened, on this day to be sent out on life's path.

Make a clear change to anything that remains from Christmas. All Christmas decorations are to be removed on the fifth except those with king and star motifs. The tree and all remaining greenery have to go. Use pictures of the *upright* infant and the baptism. Or even privately try to paint your own! This is far more effective and you may be really amazed at new insights following such as an attempt, even though you might not want straight away to show the picture to everyone else. The star is a five-pointed star, not the six-pointed Star of David, which is appropriate for Christmas. Can you draw one or walk one on the floor without breaking the line? As Epiphany is a festival of light it is worth trying to perceive how the light changes and this can be done assisted by fixing coloured paper stars to the sunlit windows. Experiment with white, yellow, orange, lilac, violet and magenta to sense which sequence best matches the changing quality of the light. Gardeners may enjoy gathering (for which they need first to have planted!) the appropriate garden flowers as they emerge. Otherwise freesias or anemones can be bought in. Let the blue cloths of Advent or Christmas with their red and green decorations disappear and let a violet or red-violet be the basis for the gold stars and crystals of the quartz family—the translucent ones, such as rock crystals, amethyst, citrine, rose quartz (as free from yellow milkiness as attainable), and smoky quartz or morion.

It is helpful to take account of the positive traits that others have attributed to us and resolve to overcome our doubts about them by strengthening them in the year to come, looking for practical areas in which they can be used or developed. Then why not choose a trait we admire in someone else because of our own lack in that direction and do the same?

Symbolism plays an important part in festivals, and finding symbols for things stimulates the artistic and imaginative faculties which are so valuable for grasping the truths of the spiritual life. So try to find or make symbols for these two attributes (our own and someone else's) and place them somewhere they can be seen daily as reminders of our resolves which already contain our own artistic will. During the month, take time to see where the kingly attributes of interest, sacrifice and love can start to work in the areas of life belonging to these two symbols. What would the people involved want or expect from a wise, benevolent king or even of a spiritual being, and can that give us any inspiration?

Closing the festival

Two important dates help us close the month of Epiphany. One is 1 February, St Bride's Day. St Bride is connected with Brighida, a Norse goddess of light, changed into the warmth of heart of the young girl Brigid Bride of Iona who became the 'foster mother of Jesus' (see the story by Fiona MacLeod). Then there is 2 February, Candlemas, which is based on the entry into the temple (Luke 2:22) of Mary and Joseph with Jesus to present their first-born and for the purification of the mother, 40 days after giving birth, to fulfil the law. The temple was originally designed as the house on Earth for the God of the I AM (Jehovah) to dwell in a spiritual and physical way. (See Solomon's prayer of consecration of the temple, 1 Kings 8:22.) Now the Son of God enters it, who later said, 'Destroy this temple and I will rebuild it in three days' (John 2:19, author's rendering) and its purpose is fulfilled.

Candle-dipping can be a personal counterpart to the Candlemas tradition of blessing church candles for the coming year, that the light of this season be also outwardly visible in the months to come. Light is referred to later in this book.

Summary

The Epiphany festival lets the qualities of what has been our spiritual rebirth during Christmastime, the Twelve Holy Days, shine out into the world, setting us out on the path of the year. Our inner life, our practical life and our social life all receive a new stimulus.

5
CANDLEMAS

2 February

Motif

Despite the theory that considers creation to be a product of randomness, not many people feel that this is plausible. It does not satisfy the folk-mind, which would rather subscribe to 'no smoke without fire', even if the fire of creation is in this case hidden. To many researchers and thinkers, nature's randomness, where it occurs, often becomes order when a greater perspective is discovered. Human beings are also able to create: they are of like 'nature' to the creator, even if the degree is astronomically less. The festivals described here are those that reveal the year as a *life* cycle of that Creator Spirit (however we want to imagine it) who then became Man. Whatever one may think of Jesus, he depicts a far greater creativity than most if not all human beings, even as far as creating a new body for the resurrection. The creator enters the temple (Luke 2:22), which is destroyed and then rebuilt in three days (John 2:19). The rituals of this cycle imbue nature (including human nature) with the gifts of resurrection. They transform and re-create out of the *dying* processes of the Earth (erosion, desert forming, etc.). To fulfil this aim we need to find for this essentially pre-Christian quarter day something in the Christian realm that is able to meet it, embrace it, and raise it to a higher wholeness. To do this we shall look at the Celtic fourfoldness of Woman.

Nature

Characteristic of this season are the clouds and the daylight. Out of the heaviness of winter, clouds can change from small, rising woolly masses to large, bright rain clouds, brilliant in the sunlight—which can be hot, calling forth the bees for exercise and fresh food. The light is still cool and crystalline; we can imagine its rays carrying down into the Earth the *spirit*-picture of the plant to come, to be united with its *life*-picture slumbering in the earth, like the light of a 'kingly' (sovereign) idea, through which we see what needs to be done. Later, at Easter, the light becomes charged with an atmosphere of feeling—but here, in February, it is still passionless and pure. The light-dark drama of Lent is still to come. It is innocent in its green clarity or orange magic on the bare ash branches at sundown, innocent on birch twigs and willow wands, turning the valleys into a transfigured earth palette.

The challenge is to remind ourselves that man's task for nature is to lift her into a new role. Our eye must shine on her like the Sun, must unveil her likeness so she can give us her material to be transformed by us in our daily tasks, giving her wholeness.

The first aspect of Candlemas is the close of the Epiphany season, so preparation begins by clearing away our Epiphany properties and trying to replace them with those of nature that have been called forth from the dark earth by the Epiphany light. Ice crystal stars become blossoms, bare twigs become flowering ones. These are not the luxuriant blooms of the spring still to come but blossoms that burst before the leaves, from the dark branch: sloe, almond, red hazel flowers and catkins, japonica and forsythia. Some crystals of the coloured quartz range still have their place in our homes: pink rose quartz, mauve amethyst and black morion. If a gnome has the chance of watching over them and taking pride in the hard work of pushing a flower out of the dark stem, or a crystal out of the ground, so he will. After all, it is only common sense to do such a thing . . .

The gnome is the elemental spirit of the earthly realm, especially where it is moist and therefore fertile. We meet him in Grimms' fairy tales, and in other folk tales, where he shows his propensities to help or hinder. See *Harmony of the Creative Word.*[12]

The gnome is the ideal person to create your festival. Bring him a nice slate tile as a base (slate is a real image of ancient creative light having become silica in primeval granite, then being washed to mud by the flood and hardened to flatness by the weight of its own matter) and let him show you where to place the crystals and branches upon it to best effect. He will want you to ensure that this little image of the young Earth is in a place where the morning sun can strike it to reveal the magic. He will himself want to stand just where he can look best and where the Sun's rays can transform his ancient beard into light. That tells him what flowers you need to pick to add in small glass vases (which will also catch the light) so that when you go into the garden to cut them you can listen out of the back of your shoulderblades or neck for his whisper and watch the ground with sharp eyes to find the right ones. If after arranging these you scatter a couple of small tumbled garnets or carnelians at his feet he will know that you are not quite as stupid as you look.

The gnome is a being invisible to physical sight and has his place where the elements of earth and water intermingle. Gnomes are active where a stone is constantly wetted so that moss may grow there. Deep in the Earth, metallic veins provide an element which is for gnomes non-material, which along with their connection with crystals gives the picture-image of a little miner. The Cornish tradition of these beings known to the tin miners was that according to their mood, or judgement on the miner, they could either hide his tools or show him where a rich vein of metal could be found.

Gnomes are beings of great intelligence but they know things without having to think them first. They just perceive them through sniffing the air of the cosmos or the metallic nerves of the Earth. (This faculty may make them rather nervy at times.) They think us rather stupid because we cannot do this, but on the other hand they are inquisitive about human life because it belongs to a world very different from theirs. For them the most puzzling thing is a young child, because it is not yet fully of the Earth; and it is said that if we want to draw near to the realm of the gnomes we must tell them stories of small children. On the other hand again, if we are going to start doing this we have to acquire a gnome faculty, namely that of wakefulness. Just as the gnome is ever wakeful to protect himself from certain gnome-risks, we have to ensure that we do not fall prey to gnome-pranks. Although intelligent, they lack morality. The phase that little boys sometimes go through of playing tricks on their sisters is not yet what we would call immoral, but if it became a permanent state we would be justified in calling it an act of immorality. So the gnome challenges us to be disciplined in ourselves so that we can anticipate the pranks like a seasoned schoolteacher and meet them with humour and control.

The little scenario described above with building the Candlemas garden in our hearts is helpful to the gnome world because gnomes appreciate some of the magic of nature with which they have been involved. Our motif of elevating nature by bringing her into our festivals also raises the existence of the gnomes into our own ken. This involvement of our hearts, will and attitude in their world sometimes has the result described above: that when we are looking for the best examples of their own work in nature, looking without intellect but with a broadness we described as being out of the space behind our head and shoulderblades instead of forwards from between our eyebrows, then we can have a sense of being helped. This may be felt as an improvement in our inner mood or some piece of outer good fortune like a good find in the garden or on the seashore or hills.

Biblical context

Candlemas falls in the midst of the 40 days in the Wilderness (6 January to 15 February) in which Jesus fasts following the baptism and, seen through Celtic eyes, encounters the Earth as the desert place it would become if he were not to embrace it and lead it over from death on Golgotha, the 'Place of a Skull', to the *garden* of the empty tomb. Candlemas is a festival in which the divine Sun-quality that has created or begotten the world out of primal dark substance now incarnates in Christ and grasps the loving female nature of the Jesus man. In so doing he unites with the light-maiden of nature (Brighida). Matthew, Mark and Luke speak of Christ's 40 days of fasting and temptations after the baptism whereas John says, 'on the third day there was a *marriage*' (John 2:1). No bride is mentioned (and the groom only to be told by the master of the feast that the 'old' wine has failed); but mysterious words pass between Jesus and his mother: 'What is to me and to thee, woman?' (verse 4, author's rendering). She says to the servants, 'Do whatever he tells you,' thus endowing Jesus with her cosmic-heavenly authority. They then draw from the earth the water that will become wine through the sunshine of that feast: sunshine of Sun-being indwelling youthful human soul in the presence of the Mother.

The four main pagan festivals follow the life phases of woman: Maiden, Bride, Mother and Crone (or Wise Woman). And this festival is that of the Maiden, the others being May Day or Beltane, Lammas or Lughnasadh and Hallowe'en or Samhain respectively. She is the maiden who is light and gay but facing the responsibilities of later life already, in caring for, say, a baby brother or, beautifully in the St Bride story, Jesus himself. Brighida, an ancient goddess of light becomes Brigid, renamed Bride, indicating the next stage of womanhood for which Brigid is being prepared. The Christian 'Book of the Dead', or Book of Revelation, describes the descent from heaven of the Future as a 'bride adorned for her husband'; and the description of this holy city is in terms of the noble representatives of the mineral and plant realms—gold, precious stones, the river of life, and the tree of life.

We have here a glimpse into the pagan or non-denominational, non-confessional aspect of Christianity. In the Gospel and Apocalypse Christ is presented as the Bridegroom, who will fructify all of human life. In pagan tradition it is the Lord of the elements, who will, as the bridegroom, take both the Earth-maiden and the youthful human soul, embrace them, conceive upon them and lead them over into fruitfulness and wisdom.

These all contain rich material that we can take in and make our own: the St Bride story (illustrating the first age of Woman, the Maiden); the story of Jesus and Simeon in the temple (Luke 2:25) (the third age, Mother); the marriage at Cana (John 2:1) (the second age, Bride), followed by the cleansing of the temple, and the new Jerusalem (Rev. 3:12; 21 and 22). (For the fourth age, Wise Woman, we may wait for the Woman under the Cross on Good Friday, for Whitsun, among the disciples and for Hallowe'en). Then we may remember the 'gnome' featured above and 'feed' him their fruits. This will then enhance his future work in helping human beings grasp the mysteries of the marriage of spiritual sunlight to the pure, maidenly potential of the Earth and the untapped resources of their own nature. When no one else is listening, you can read some of these texts to him. You may feel a bit weird doing this but it is worth a try!

Another activity for Candlemas, if you have the time, is candle making. You can either use up all the wax saved from previous months or acquire some fresh wax. Beeswax is ideal for this purpose. Using moulds can be quite difficult—simpler ways are dipping and rolling. To dip candles you will need a deep tin (catering tins of olive oil or golden syrup are ideal) and some candlewick, which is obtainable at craft shops and usually marked by the thickness of the candle for which it is designed. Use an old saucepan large enough to hold the base of the tin. Pour some boiling water into the bottom of the saucepan, place the wax in the tin and put the whole on heat until it is melted (allow plenty of time for this). You can also pour hot water on the wax, so that it melts and floats, but if that water is too hot it will spoil the wax. (Heating the wax without water or a water bath is a fire risk). When the wax is just molten, dip in a length of wick for a few seconds, just long enough for it to absorb the wax, then lift it out to cool. Each time this is repeated your candle will grow. You can hold one wick in each hand or you can tie two or three wicks to each of two short sticks and hold one of them in each hand and alternate the dipping. When the candle is thick enough, while it is still warm, cut off some of the base with a sharp knife until the bottom of the wick is visible.

To roll candles, first dip a length of wick once as above and let it harden straight. Choose a sheet of beeswax of your choice and roll it around the wick, using further sheets until the desired thickness is reached. Find these sheets in a craft shop or obtain from a beekeeping supplier (where you can also buy them already moulded for honeycomb). Using these with a particular thickness of wick you need to make the candles a third thicker to compensate for the air spaces in the impressed sheets.

If you do want to use moulds, wipe them inside with washing-up liquid.

Using these candles at, say, All Souls (see p. 121) brings a memory of the growing sunlight into the season of increasing darkness (Northern Hemisphere!).

Meditative pictures

1. The 40 days in the Wilderness and the temptations of Christ (Matt. 4:1; Mark 1:12; Luke 4:1), because these follow the baptism with:
2. The transformation of groundwater into grape juice in the vine between Sun and Earth and in the ritual vessels of the wedding feast between Jesus, his mother and the community (John 2:1). 'On the third day' the marriage shows Jesus as he is *after* the trials of the temptations.
3. Above is the Sun, below is the Earth; on the Earth are plants and within the Earth are crystals. Imagine a plant germinating, growing, blossoming, seeding and fading. The Earth-being senses its glory and treasures it in its decline. The Sun-being invests the seed as it falls into the Earth-womb.
4. Sun-glory and Earth-glory lighten up at Candlemas as a *parable* of what is otherwise spread through space and time: the Earth's life over the whole year (plants germinate or fade throughout the year) and over the whole planet.
5. The ritual sacrifice of the innocent dove (Luke 2:24) in the temple served to restore maiden purity to Mary 40 days after giving birth. In non-Christian language this is Maya, the Earth Maiden and Mother-to-Be, whose cloak is the sense world of nature in all its seasonal splendour; for what we see with our eyes is the covering of a host of forces and beings—with the primal Goddess behind them all.

6. St Bride, as recounted in the story retold by Fiona MacLeod as taking place at the time of Christ between Iona, Bethlehem and the Mount of Olives, could, in her innocence, become the 'foster mother of Christ' without leaving behind her maidenhood. Now this Jesus-child of 40 days, who shall become the Lord of the elements, the bearer of the life cycles and processes of the Earth, is brought into the *human* temple. The male force of the sky is united with the matrix form of the Earth, to bear a new humanity through which a 'new heaven and a new earth' (Rev. 21:1) can come about.

   Think of this in parallel with 3 and 4 above.

Prayer

The classic prayer of Simeon (Luke 2:29) can move us at this time: 'Lord, let now your servant depart in peace, for my eyes have seen your healing work'—healing work of salvation for the Earth-soul and our own soul. We can also pray by looking at our year ahead for our personal challenges and call for light to shine on us all like a consecrated candle.

A special mood of prayer is generated by some of the last sentences of the New Testament, 'See, I am coming soon, bringing my recompense, to fulfil for everyone the destiny of what he has done. I am the Alpha and the Omega, the first and the last, the beginning and the end. Blessed are those who cleanse their garments (through prayer), that they may have the right to the tree of life . . .' (Rev. 22:12, author's rendering.)

Contemplation of nature—in northern and southern continents

What a wide range of natural backgrounds prevail around the world at this time, from dry autumn to monsoon torrents—drought or drowning! The Sun is in the Waterman both in the Northern and Southern Hemispheres, and at night the Milky Way shines in the South with the amazing contrast of its bright star clouds and dark starless spaces, a totally different experience from that in the Northern Hemisphere. Here the challenge is to see which phenomena carry the main gesture of the *season* and to relate them to the stories (Gospel or other) the northern gnome (or festival genius) likes to hear best. The question is: do the southern gnomes like the same stories or different ones? Our thesis is to tell them the *same* ones and let them act from them into nature out of their *own* wisdom and responsibilities, for they are ruled by the same Waterman Sun as in the north and the same constellations of Moon and planets. Christ has incarnated through one 'birth horoscope', or starry juxtaposition. He has lived and does still live and work as Earth Spirit, now not *out* of a certain horoscope but *into* it. He projects his work from the Earth centre out into the cosmos, teaching the cosmos its new astrology. Gnomes know this: they have their annual Christmas synod with their elemental lord. They expect us to use Earth intelligence and 'one-Earth' stories and festivals in which they can participate, to prevent the Earth becoming divided in herself. This thesis is not presented as a dogma but as something on which to meditate. The author is aware just how complex this whole question is and how much research over how long a time will be needed in order to move towards an answer. May what is written here be a contribution in this quest.

Northern Territory Australians know the 'Lightning Man' or Namarrgon, a Dreamtime being, whose semen is the thunder-rain—the drops of life-giving water cast fresh out of the spiritual-etheric core of the cloud—which fructifies the earth.

Creating your festival

The Celtic festival of Imbolc celebrated Maidenhood or the First Age of Woman in connection with the Earth's unfolding of its own first growth. The traditional rhyme

> If Candlemas Day be fair and bright
> Winter will have another flight
> But if it be dark with clouds and rain
> Winter is gone, and will not come again.

shows its transitional place between winter and spring. Spring is not just given—it needs working for; the old pagan rituals would serve this end, for example through sacrifices, to nourish nature for her renewed unfolding.

This festival may last two or three days or a whole month, depending on our inclination and the timing of Easter. March already brings in a new mood, wherever one is in the world. At the latest however, a change needs to be made to our festive table before the beginning of Lent. The best guide is our inner feeling and our awareness of the quality of light in the unfolding or the inward-turning year. We may also choose to have a festival-free period at this point.

Summary

Lighting a candle creates a special moment of expectancy. We do not light candles without reason. We do it to enhance the mood and to achieve this we select a candle most suitable for the occasion—a tall thin one or a short thick one or ones of different colours. Nowadays there is also a wide choice of perfume that can fill the room while the candle is burning. However, it may be that at Candlemas, working with a feeling for consecrating candles for the year, we want to choose a natural perfume from a natural form of wax; and it is beeswax that combines both, requiring as it does the minimum of preparation for candle making, leaving it close to nature. Its light creates a wonderful, glowing space, which we can enter, as though entering a temple.

All through the previous summer, flowers have blossomed and the Sun has called forth from deep within them the nectar that the bees harvest. It is their nourishment and they render it into honey to nourish themselves further, but they also make it into beeswax for building their home, the 'body' of their colony. Nature has so ordained it that bees, like other creatures, produce a natural surplus, not only one of honey but also of wax, which is a memory in substance of the relationship between the light and warmth of the Sun and the beauty and fruitfulness of the Earth.

Lighting a candle releases these images in our imagination if we have chosen our candle with them in mind. And this consecrates our candle, for our imagination then meets the aroma of the burning wax and the warm light being shed around it and us, building a temple whose material is natural light and whose architecture mental light. ('Consecration' is the uniting of something with its living origin or archetype.)

In this way we are carrying the life of one year into the next. What Sun and Earth had produced together we have harvested and brought forward as an enhancement of the life of our festivities in the present and future.

But it is not only in this way that this enhancement is possible. Whatever we are going to do that is important to us or that we know is important to somebody else can be prepared by remembering those fruits of the past, which we have been given through the interplay of what is of Earth with what is of Heaven. Remembering the blessings of the past while we prepare a step into the future is also a consecration of our deeds; we kindle an inner light through our expectancy of doing good. Those who will participate in our actions—we are perhaps allowed to hope—will absorb our inner warmth and be enlightened by our inner light. Our life-arena becomes a temple ...

We sometimes say of someone's wonderful achievement, 'I couldn't hold a candle to that'—but perhaps the spirit of Candlemas will enable us to achieve such a wonder in the future. For is not the candle an image of our own self, born out of the interplay of Earth and Heaven, with a straightness inside it? Simeon in the temple is described as 'righteous'. In this context righteousness means to be inwardly straight. When he sees the Child of Heaven he feels that his life has reached its fulfilment, for his own straightness has touched the straightness of the world.

And when *we* enter *our* temple of prayer or light, aware of the temple of our body, is it not in the Spirit of the Universe, which we consciously and freely call down into ourselves as the motivation of our deeds, that we consecrate ourselves and bless the world? The maiden soul in us has given birth and is purified.

6
LENT

Ash Wednesday to Holy Saturday

Motif

To prepare for Easter we would do well to face the tension between our *ideals* and the *reality* of our shortcomings: 'The good that I would I do not: but the evil which I would not, that I do' (Paul, Rom. 7:19). This is sometimes *felt* as a kind of ache in the human breast as though there were an infirmity of *heart* or a weakness in *breath*.

Christ was deserted and died alone. Lent is the chance to redress this by reaching out to him in our *imagination*.

Christ died at the hands of the fallen nature of humanity—which was not originally Man's fault but a gift of *freedom*. He came to Man to give life back to him. A more sublime arrangement can scarcely be imagined.

'Lent' derives from a Germanic word for spring: it can now be loosed from the season outside to become part of the seasons of the human soul.

Nature

Early morning: there is a mist, a coolness in the air, a feeling of autumn; light is weakening day by day, warmth decreasing, and it is three weeks to Easter. We are in the Southern Hemisphere ... The mood is one of gratitude for the warmth there was and the realization: now I ought to provide my own warmth and inner light but I am not able to. There is instead an awareness of something within that hinders its own effort. The human soul is used to living between sufficiency and inadequacy but now it is our *constitution* that is felt as inadequate and gripped by darkness.

Early morning: there is a mist, a mildness in the air, birdsong is extravagant. Spring is here with its promise of light, warmth and fresh colour. The body grows younger and lighter; the soul is awakened. Easter is coming but something hinders me in my depths from *taking it for myself*. There is a shadow in the soul, an inertia in the body, despite its freshness; there can be a doubt in the mind about one's future, how far one measures up to what one believes oneself to be or what, perhaps, ought to be.

Biblical context

Early morning: is today really Good Friday? Did it really happen—the agony, the trial, the nailing up? And how did it come about, such a bizarre thing, the Creator executed by his creatures? And how quietly does the Sun shine between 12.00 and 3.00, nature holding breath. Where is Easter now, on this day, how far away?

So wherever we are on the Earth, Easter comes primarily as an *inner* challenge. Nature usually follows if given a lead, but she cannot lead *here* because the purpose of Easter was to give *her* (and Man alongside) something missing in both: the capacity to renew existence.

The history of the crucifixion of the creator of the world is well enough documented in the Gospel, but virtually nowhere else. There is no proof, but Luke wrote his Gospel so that the reader may learn how well founded is the teaching (Luke 1:4); and John wrote *his* in such a way that the reader might develop a new perception in his heart which could let him feel the reality of the events described, and thereby have life (John 20:31). The Gospel thus opens the way for us into the inmost depths of our soul and places alongside all the doubts and shadows (even iniquities) that hide there its images of the suffering and death of Jesus Christ. Thence it places alongside our mortality the death of the cross until it can open its images of resurrection, placing them in our soul if we but make space for them so that it can become part of the resurrection, as a new creation, a new human being, the Easter man.

Paul wrote about this to the Romans: we are baptized into the *death* of Christ (Rom. 6:1–4) and to the Corinthians (1 Cor. 15:42–7). Many of his words have become empty phrases now but their power can be rediscovered when the reader has really confronted death and evil in his own life, has felt guilty and helpless, has then in the end reached out for help and decided to go by choice the path of suffering which Jesus took and whose death was brought about by just those forces in human nature which are described here. This path and its treading is what is here called Lent.

In the early church people could sense the resurrection by listening to the spoken word of the apostles, and by breaking bread with those who had done the same with the Messiah before his death and after his resurrection. In Holy Week (the Sunday to Saturday before Easter) people were prepared and baptized ('baptized into the death of Christ') and then confirmed at Easter. Therefore, the days before Easter were associated with this self-knowledge and the new 'Christians' then resolved to serve the new 'creation' of transformed humanity and nature. This is called the 'Kingdom of Heaven', and is, however, on the Earth and not somewhere else: 'look, the kingdom of heaven is in the midst of you' (Luke 17:20–1)—in the midst of those walking the hard path.

Meditative pictures

Myths and legends in any culture of how death and evil have entered humanity and caused the loss of the primal state of grace.
Biographies which describe the struggle with these same forces.
Read the actual Gospel accounts of the last week of Jesus' life—easy enough to find in most New Testaments—rather than secondary texts or relying on memory. In particular:

Anointing of Jesus' feet—John 12:3
Anointing of Jesus' head—Matthew 26:6; Mark 14:3
Anointing of the body—John 19:39
Further anointing intended—Mark 16:1; Luke 24:1;
and from the Old Testament:

Psalm 8: 'O Lord our Lord . . . What is man?'
Psalm 39: 'I will watch how I behave'
Psalm 40: 'I waited patiently for the Lord'
The story of Jonah . . . 'The waters closed in over me'—Jonah 2:5.

Prayer

May what Christ has begun be continued through human effort.
May space be made in humanity for the grace of the Creator's death and resurrection to take root there, that he find a place there to be a redeemer of our nature and a working partner in our own redemptive efforts.
Psalm 22: 'My God, my God why have you forsaken me?' (author's rendering)

Psalm 23: 'The Lord is my shepherd'
John 12:27: 'Now is my soul troubled'
John 17: 'Father, the hour has come; reveal your Son' (author's rendering)

Contemplation of nature—in northern and southern continents

Nature—north

We can feel a tension between the onrush of spring and the lack of warmth; then also in the play of brightness and shadiness in the clouds as they change rapidly. Our soul can become out of balance in joy and sorrow. Though nature is also full of nourishment for the soul, there is no stable balance yet. To find a spirit of balance as depicted in the scales of Michaelmas (Libra) is the challenge for the soul living in Lent. This is strengthened by watching the earthly colours of the buds change the colour face of the woodlands and hedges until, piecemeal, the green breaks out—this furnishes an inner and more stable warmth through its beauty. So the moving balance we experience in the action of walking can begin to work up into our pulse and breath, to be met there at Easter with a healing that works down from our head as light and blissful warmth to come.

Nature—south

We may well find that the signs of autumn are only in decreasing light, warmth, mist and dew and that the 'Fall' of leaves really only applies to plants in (or from) the Northern Hemisphere. Many indigenous plants have started to renew their foliage at Epiphany and are now coming into blossom. The variety of southern nature is simply too great to generalize about, but the Sun is nonetheless moving lower in the sky and asking us to think of the *true* origin of death and its overcoming rather than just its cyclical and therefore impermanent manifestation in nature. Nature offers sights of both growing and of dying; just as in the north the snowdrops go to seed in Lent, in the south the challenge is to bring these observations into a whole and ask what the Earth needs to lead her forwards to a new existence rather than go the way of modern cosmological models (i.e. the death of the universe). How can Man husband her in this direction if not through Lent and Easter?

Pastoral interlude: the water being or undine

The river winds its way down the valley under early spring light. As the wind brushes the clouds, the Sun shines through, giving colour to the grey of the heather and the wet grass. The air smells of future growth, as though the ground itself was about to stir into creation.

A larch tree hangs over a bend in the river. Its long fine branches reach towards the water and small bursts of lightest green spring from them. The water flows deep there, beneath the bank.

When you stand and look through the shadow of the tree you see the sunlit grass beyond reflect itself in the moving, mottling water. The green tresses of the tree sway in the breeze that shivers the surface of the water. Then, when you stop thinking, you will see through the green, the ripples, the swaying, the sunlight shifting in and out—you will see a movement that distils itself out of the living air and fills the water with being, fills the moving stillness with creative urge.

The water-maiden rises out of the gentle flood up into the green light that enwraps her flowing form in a green and silver shimmer. The little scarlet buds of the larch decorate her green hair like garnets. Her eyes dream towards you—her gaze will dissolve you if you gaze back too long. Then you hear the silver voice of the depths that rises with longing into the light, longing to create the green, to generate the green of the world, of the valley, longing to draw the light and weave tone-melodies into it to beget the delicate substance of leaf in this crucible of water and light.

You will remember this forever. And you will return in hope, but you will never see again—you will only feel the longing. For the apparition is a dream in your mind that you saw with your eye and heard with your ear—the sound of the ache to create, to vanish in the doing. So now: create the leaf there yourself, then another and another, all along the stem. Let the breeze blow through the leaves of your mind until all the watery melody of the maiden is absorbed into the foliage of the spring world and shot through with airy light and she is taken up into the arms of the warming air and transformed into a calyx, to reveal all beauty into the higher realm of blossom. Then your longing—hers too!—will be stilled in the grace of doing.

The gnome visited us in the chapter on Candlemas; now this is the 'undine'. This is the elemental being of the water, especially where it is moved by air. We can think of the spray of a waterfall, the spume of the breaking wave or the beautiful delicate colours of fish scales.

Whilst spiritual science is sensitive to the places where rock is wetted by water for the activity of the gnomes, so it finds the activity of the water spirits, or undines, where water is activated by air, like the ripples caused by the breeze or by air bubbling through the water. What is here seen plainly in the elements themselves is repeated in an advanced way in the plant leaf. The leaves, moved into life by the breeze, are largely composed of water (in compound with carbon); and it is known that their substance is created by a metabolism of light. Here, the undines are active in photosynthesis or plant chemistry, but they do this in cooperation with the next group of elemental beings, who live in the element of air, warm air. The undine likes to balance the raindrops with the sunlight and the moist gaps in the fluffy rainclouds to provide the material for the spirits of the air to let the rainbow colours play across the sky. Undines appear in folk tales for good or ill, always connected to the magic and mystery of water—pools, streams, springs and the breaking waves. They strive upwards to the light around the cliffs of Tintagel (amongst others) and appear to sea folk in female guise.

We will meet the air spirits, and learn more about their cooperation with the undines, in a later chapter. Very methodical accounts of all these beings are to be found in Rudolf Steiner's lectures.[13]

Creating your festival

Lent was established by the church as a time of penance but did not include the Sundays in its 40 days. Shrove Tuesday, the day beforehand, was for being absolved or 'shriven' through confession, so the path to Easter would be clearer. And in Lent one avoided those things which weigh or sully body and soul and affirmed those that build up the character. Our own self-knowledge can suggest to us what we might undertake in terms of abstinence (of certain foods, pleasures, negative thoughts or moods, etc.) not as mortification to convince oneself one is a good person but to strengthen one's will-power, and increase self-discipline and control over one's own bodily and soul nature.

One can also learn to appreciate small pleasures and ask how they can be helped to grow until there is a surplus available for others.

In the positive direction, it is a good time to take on a change of habit. For example, try changing your handwriting or phrases you use. Or choose to use fashionable idioms for their own linguistic merit rather than to be fashionable oneself. Or perhaps adopt a leaner diet. It is amazing what can be achieved over three or four years through these few weeks of Lenten discipline. One can also focus on the four weeks before Easter rather than the full seven—a shorter all-out effort is often more successful than a longer failure. What goes on in the hands, tongue and digestion certainly affects one's ability to develop the right *heart* faculty that Easter relies on to enter our soul. A good area of study is that of the human being himself. What is really known now for certain, rather than as hypothesis or research model? Is Man *determined* by genes, imitation, environment? And where is he not so? Is Man just a body with a pump and computer inserted? If not, how does one know? Is the Earth just a lump of hot iron with air and water around it? Is the Earth a fallen being, needing uplift? Such considerations prepare our insight into the mysteries of that complex creation, the resurrection body of Man.

Working from the above, project what one is attempting out into one's home. Clear out dirt and dross. Discipline the room. Let meals reflect this too, especially in Holy Week and then especially on the Thursday—Maundy Thursday—remembering the Holy Supper.

Follow in the Gospel what Christ did during those days and try to find someone with whom to share this. (For references see the table below.)

Summary

Lent unfolds in stages that become ever more concentrated. Seven weeks before, from the Sunday before Shrove Tuesday, our thoughts begin to focus on Lent and Easter. Four weeks before, feelings increase towards the plight of the inner man and the problem of coming to terms with our nature and the situation in the world around. And one week before, the daily events of the primal 'Holy' Week are well taken into the depths of human souls. Three days before, people break bread and share grape juice in memory of a farewell meal between Jesus and those who are to join his work in their own lives and for whom he prays (John 17:20). Then we finally reach the day of death, Good Friday, and its three special hours, 12–3. Then comes Holy Saturday, silent as the grave, the day of rest after the first creation (Gen. 2:1–3): Earth and Man wait for the tomb to be broken open. The close of Lent is really Holy Saturday. The more death is experienced beforehand, the more the first week of the new creation can be just that; one can look back to Lent out of the newly opened world of a life that will continue beyond the end of the physical Earth and bears in the Gospel the allegorical name Galilee. 'There you will see him as he told you' (Mark 16:7).

Gospel readings describing the days of Holy Week

Day	Matthew	Mark	Luke	John
Sunday	21:1–11	11:1–11	19:28–38 (39–46*)	12:12–50
Monday	21:12–17	11:12–19	(*)	—
Tuesday	21:18–46 22 23 24 25 26:1–5	11:20–33 12 13	19:47 20 21	—
Wednesday	26:6–16	14:1–11	22:1–6	—
Thursday	26:17–35	14:12–31	22:7–38	13 14 15 16 17
Friday	26:36–75 27:1–66	14:32–72 15	22:39–71 23	18 19
Saturday	—	—	23:56	—
EASTER	28:1–15	16:1–8	24:1–43	21

* It is unclear whether these passages refer to Sunday or Monday. There could easily have been a Temple cleansing on both days. It is also not easy to fix the fig-tree narrative to one particular day. The more one lives with the Gospels the more one attains the heart perception generated and awakened through their words—the less vital it is to reach an intellectually watertight 'reason' in them. Their life-content becomes 'knowledge' in its own right, of a kind that brings one closer to their mysteries than the senses and intellect can or even should do.

7
EASTER

Easter Day, for 40 Days

Motif

It was said that Good Friday is historical. Ormond Edwards[14] corroborates by historical means the date given from the spiritual research of Rudolf Steiner, namely 3 April in the year 33. The background to this speaks a strong language. The Jewish festival of Passover was established by Jehovah as the culmination of the struggle between Moses and Pharaoh (see Exod. 12:2). This depicts a representative of those people chosen later to witness Easter striving against the powers of hindrance which would fetter human beings in slavery. Each family slaughtered a pure lamb from its flock, marked the doorposts and lintels with its blood and ate the lamb in a solemn meal in readiness for flight. The angel of death came that night and slew every first-born male—human and animal—but 'passed over' the marked houses. The Israelites were saved. Jesus enters Jerusalem at the beginning of this festival 1300 years later. He himself becomes the sacrificial lamb, the one man without personal sin, the God who was creator become creature (Man). This is to cleanse human nature from the constitutional 'sin' or illness which causes it to be mortal and fallible. He is sacrificed on a cross just at the time the Passover lambs were slaughtered in the temple. His blood reaches the Earth at the same time as theirs. So Easter is an octave of Passover: from freedom from tyranny through sacrificing an earthly lamb, to freedom from the inner power of death through God sacrificing his son, *the* Lamb.

Christianity is the religion that bears witness to this. Judaism contains a minority who join this witness also. The majority still await it. Islam seems to go a different path altogether.

The last innate possibility withers away, and a new beginning comes from a different angle, empowered by gentle, commanding love.

The name Jehovah, 'I am I who was and is and will be', contains both these extremes at once. That is its power. Easter is the festival during which this principle descends to Earth, beginning at the baptism and culminating in the resurrection. The individual seeds of this transformation can then be sown elsewhere to enliven what is not yet at the point of dying. The Kingdom of Heaven is like leaven (Matt. 13:33; Luke 13:21). Easter saves the life of the human being and the Earth. But what mankind will do with this redemption is not yet certain.

Nature

Our approach is that nature is renewed by Christianity. Easter is the beginning of this, so 'local' nature is the *least* relevant. We have seen the stark contrast between spring and Lent. This chapter includes some observations on light and warmth and how these elements weave a matrix for sensing the resurrection.

Biblical context

Although fundamental to Christianity, Easter itself is neither historical nor 'natural'. It is traditional to celebrate Easter on the Sunday following the spring Full Moon, but there is no historical proof of the resurrection. It is unlikely too that there ever will be, for even St Paul offers no historical proof. Whatever our background—agnostic, Christian, or other religion or philosophy—we are faced with the question of where to start. The proof is in the experience, but how is this to be obtained? It is certain that the resurrection can be disproved and the Gospels discredited. That is an important clue to the true nature, true *substance* of this experience.

There is personal activity that can produce fruits whose qualities simply bear no comparison with those of outer proofs because they *nourish*. There are historical cases for dating Christmas and Epiphany, even Good Friday,[15] but to grasp Easter requires a preparedness to *change oneself*, and this is the stated purpose of that unique text the 'Gospel according to John'. This is the starting point recommended here: 'There are many things that Jesus did that are not recorded in this book but these are written that you may believe that Jesus is the Messiah [i.e. the Christ = the anointed one] the Son of God, and that, believing, you may have life in his name' (John 20:30–1). One is invited to change oneself by meditating the pictures of this Gospel and essentially let them grow from one to the next to open up the heart that has been closed to heaven in infancy to prepare for living in the sense world. The heart awakens to another kind of knowing, akin to intuition, which can receive and relate to another being. Looking at someone's clothing tells us something about them, but it is not them. Looking at someone's face tells much more, but it is still not them. Looking through their eyes into their soul is again more, but it is not yet their *eternal* being. It is in receiving what they *do* that lets us come closer still. Consider treasuring a poem; a poem is not *proof* of anything but conveys substance. The Gospel is not proof but also conveys substance. The Gospel in which the writer, referring to himself, says, 'he who saw it bears witness and he himself knows that he speaks true, that you might believe' provides just such a substance. And his witness *is* true (John 19:35). Truth is *alethia*, that which overcomes the power of Lethe, the river of forgetfulness of such things as this. This, as it stands, is far from logical ('this is true because I say so and we know that I'm telling the truth'). Yet how else is one to speak if one has oneself been raised from the dead and then beheld him who has raised one then raise himself? Grasping Easter means working for this inner perception, which can come to all at the right moment for them, and then applying the experience to the created world as a seed. Easter can feed the earth because the experience Easter is the *opposite* of natural. The result, if it may be stated simply, is that this experience remains through our own death and lights up the darkness that otherwise holds sway there. Nature needs Easter for her own resurrection as does Man for his. Easter changes radically the relationship of the human being to nature. It emancipates him from her in order that *he* can bear *her* further. Celebrating festivals in the way meant in this book is an important way of making this real. The true festival is an extension of the Gospel of witness as quoted above. It takes some of nature's substance through the living forms of her bounty and informs, imbues it with the substance of resurrection by re-forming, composing nature's parts into a picture of resurrection. The inner ability to create this kind of composition is awakened through the compositional element of John's Gospel. This ability is mysteriously called faith. In the festival, nature and human are reunited. Nature has been raised by us into our own emancipation. Christian festivals must not fall back to being mere nature festivals. They must *nourish*.

Meditative pictures

The biblical context showed Easter as something from the 'beyond' which is taking hold gradually of the whole of life on Earth after its once and great inception in one human being. It was said that the series of pictures in the Gospel were written especially by John to help us to an inner experience of the content, by *living into their sequence*. This effort is deepened by meditation, the total union of the soul with each picture, letting it colour itself with the feelings the soul is able to lend it (which will grow from year to year). It can be much enhanced by studying Rudolf Steiner's contributions to them, in many of his lectures, though this study should not become a store of facts and used as though they were a proof, which will not lead anywhere. The process needs to be a meditative one.

1. The most basic image is that of the dying man on the cross becoming the living man with his greeting of peace. To this can be added the fact that he also reveals himself to certain souls today.
2. Further content can be to differentiate the days, then hours, leading up to the crucifixion and the days of Christ amongst his disciples after the resurrection and before the ascension, although this would be better attempted spread over that same 40-day period in which it originally took place rather than at one 'sitting'. Ample material is available in the Gospel.
3. On another level, details not recorded elsewhere may be allowed to arise out of the enquiring mind and artistic feeling: the tomb in the rock, as Grave of the Earth; the body collapsing in death, the wrappings falling softly into a heap. What kind of substance really fell from there into the opened earth, the dust of death and leaven of life? In the darkness of the tomb there is a stirring. How did he see the inside the tomb, the world outside as the stone was displaced? How was it to walk the garden of the Earth with feet that had in life (but which now must be regarded as death) not only been nailed but previously anointed? How did he walk in the times not described? Did he wash the disciples' feet to the same end? And what about our feet?

   Gospel accounts of meetings with him may likewise be meditated from his side as well as ours.

4. The most simple and perhaps most telling: on Easter Day, look back from the mood of that day to remember in meditation what the heart felt on Good Friday. One of the central Christian

meditations is that of the Rose Cross: seven red roses around the centre of a black cross. For the building up and practice of this meditation, see *Occult Science*.[16]

5. An Aboriginal story uses the transition from caterpillar to butterfly to depict and convey the overcoming of death. Does it not lead the soul to see into the world of life beyond the Earth, enfolding it and penetrating it where conditions are right?
6. We look at a corpse, remembering a life, remembering the increasing struggles with illness, cantankerousness even to the point of nastiness. Was this really our dear friend or relative? Suddenly a climax, then a breakthrough: no more pain! The medical staff could not explain, some of the nurses understood, a radiance grows benignly for all who visit. The fruit is ripe and falls without a sound in peace. 'I'm ready to go home now.'
7. A bright child grows, succeeds at school and work and raises a family. A brain tumour strikes. Beauty is distorted, intelligence gone, sitting and sitting ... gazing. But, after some years, have our thoughts in the orbit of that life grown in inner stature because of it? Has someone here made a sacrifice for our own growth or inner life?
8. Or the mind remains, but the body is crippled. After some years, has the person grown in inner stature? Or have they fallen and, if so, why?
9. The painting has been going well and is nearly finished until a bad stroke darkens it. The painter makes an inner adjustment and works with the mistake: a light enters the picture out of that darkness. The work is no longer 'beautiful'. Its beauty died into the darkness and rose again as nourishing good.
10. The relationship seems to be at an end. The original hopes have been destroyed or starved to death. There are no new ideas ... But what is the world needing from that relationship? Fresh buds grow from nowhere on a small green patch on the old wood. The green patch was not there to the gaze of those whose relationship had become old wood—someone gave it to them, or opened their eyes!
11. Beyond the desert is a green hill with trees and morning dew. The Sun rises over the scene of sorrow. But 'he is not here' (Mark 16:6). 'The cross on Golgotha cannot redeem you from

evil unless it be erected also within you' (Angelus Silesius).[17] 'There you will see him as he told you' (Mark 16:7).

12. A closed room, men wondering all night fruitlessly about the future. The early hours—quiet outside, empty hearts and stomachs—then a change of mood. There is a feeling of the open sea slowly approaching the shore of a new day—someone there. It is the bread breaker, the giver of fish, the giver of peace, the giver of fruitful work, the pointer of the way. (John 21.)
13. We look at a corpse—and see the pointer of the way.

Prayer

Prayer is primarily an activity of doing rather than thinking. Both realms need warmth of feeling, in this case that of Easter joy. Easter prayers, then, can be aimed at changing something in the world—which as far as our own world is concerned will be looked at in 'creating your festival'—and thus now ask for a deed for the rest of the world. So one can pray that all of humanity is helped to hear the inner 'shalom', 'salaam', 'peace be with you' (John 20:19, 26; John 14:27) that all of humanity make the step from the letter of religious doctrine to the reality of the inner empty tomb. This could be concentrated in the line of the Lord's Prayer 'Give us this day our daily bread', for it is the breakfast bread of the lakeside scene (see Meditative pictures 12 above, John 21) which opens the heart to this word. It feeds.

One can also pray that Christians worldwide could celebrate Easter together on the same (movable) date. This would surely help those of other religions or none to their own experience of Easter as we have presented it: independent of race or creed. A further prayer could be based on John 20:21, 'As the Father has sent me so do I send you.' Where is one to be sent? For what? What have I to offer? And to whom?

Contemplation of nature—in northern and southern continents

It may by now be clear that the author lays much value in finding Easter as an experience beyond nature, although one that relates to her as a renewer. Our contemplations of nature are therefore especially in those areas where she acts as *parable* for the Easter process or where she can show forth that she is changed.

Light not only fills space from Sun or atmosphere and lets us see how objects relate spatially to one another but can also radiate from the human soul through the eye. Light is such a refined, sensitive element at the edge of the sense world that it is used to refer to things of thought or spirit. 'I see the light' is not referring to daylight or anything else sense-perceptible. It is purely a supersensible or spiritual process. However, once I have seen the light supersensibly I can start to see it in the sense world. My inner experience of Easter can be seen in the outer light. I may not be able to photograph this but if *I* look at something with new eyes and see it differently why should not the gaze of the *Easter spirit* also change the light so I can see it? Like the Gospel reports, this can only be *dis*proved until we have discovered the realm in which it is true, indeed the realm which its truth has created. Search carefully through the year for the qualities of daylight, dawn, noon, dusk and starlight nature.

The parable of Easter is the dawn of these qualities. Light phenomena will show a change dependent on the festival and not on the season, for example an Easter light as distinct from a spring light. This can be practised if one has gone out upon Easter morning to watch the sunrise (parable) but only sees grey drizzle—can one see there the Easter light nonetheless?

The other element of nature to contemplate is that of warmth. This too is a link-element between nature and spirit. We can warm up our cold feet by contemplating certain thoughts in the right way—it is a totally different experience from that of a hot water bottle. Thus does the Easter event release a warmth into the world, but one of a unique quality, one that can fill the heart. Warmth in nature behaves differently in different countries, even localities. Seen simply this has much to do with the humidity there, but more accurately it is more to do with the whole interrelationship of water, earth and air into which it wants to flow or radiate.

Note: There is a significant difference between the re-emergence of life after winter, where winter is regarded as a death and spring as a resurrection, and the *great* metamorphosis—the non-natural or even *super*-natural one between Good Friday and Easter.

Northern Hemisphere

Here, both light and warmth are on the increase, but they both fluctuate considerably in springtime. How easily are we able to say of a cold east wind after a warm spell 'we are now exchanging our warmth with less fortunate parts of the hemisphere'. Then we can quickly feel the challenge to be able to give that subtle warmth out to the world and Man whatever the weather.

Southern Hemisphere

Not only human beings celebrate Easter. Nature spirits living in and through water, air and earth wait for the rising of the Fire King also.

There can be new blades of corn coming up as parable—or new, fresh 'autumn' growth after a parching summer. Or one can see a golden glow in the air to meet our Easter rejoicing, for it shows a ripeness in the realm of earth which makes visible the leavening power of the new life of the original Easter.

In the south, it is more straightforward to grasp Easter in the autumn—such as it is, for in some lands of the Southern Hemisphere autumn is mainly to be remarked in those plants and trees imported from Europe—for Christ brought resurrection into a dying world.

The real challenge is where we are penetrating parts of the Earth that have not yet experienced Christianity through human agency, even if the birds who sang on Easter morning in Jerusalem may have found their way to South Africa or Australia and taught the same melodies there. People who have stepped off a tourist car park into a jungle, desert or bush, or onto an icefield, have felt the presence of a power that could annihilate them in a trice were consciousness to be but momentarily dimmed.

In this collection the challenge in southern lands is to strip off the veneer of Europe to relate to nature, to notice for example in Australia the eucalyptus trees blooming at Easter, then on the other hand to look hard at the way European nature really is behaving there, for example, at how the trees grow, the herbs smell, the animals thrive. And into all this can be poured the Easter that is being discovered within our own soul.

Creating your festival

We recall that Easter is not a one-day festival but 39 days. Forty is the number for a new impulse to be worked out on Earth: 40 days in the ark, 40 years in the wilderness, 40 weeks of human gestation. Here, the 40th day is Ascension Day (see next chapter). We can take this period in three fortnights and say, first, Easter is in pictures: the empty tomb, the upper room—outer and inner pictures of the same events of Easter Day. We can celebrate this by rearranging something in the physical world according to our aesthetic grasp of what resurrection means. If we had a Lenten garden we can change something in it to express the above motifs. Then we can try (this is less easy!) to rearrange artistically something in our own life, our inner life, our biography. Resuming enjoyment of something given up in Lent is not meant here, but rather rearranging it to make a free, expressive contribution to our inner picture. This could mean making ourselves more aware of those areas of life that have slipped into custom and perhaps making changes to bring life up to the level of our new values. It may not be easy to make the enjoyment of coffee or chocolate an expression of freedom from 'sin', but to take into that epicurean realm and through to our social behaviour, the image of Thomas (John 20:28) 'My Lord and my God' would be like adding a new colour to our soul palette which would inspire us to repaint our whole life.

Secondly, Easter moves from the realm of picture-scene to parable—from pictures which furnish us with more definite feelings to narratives of parable or fairy-tale quality. They convey clear feelings and 'imaginations', that is whole areas of wisdom contained in one living dramatic narrative. Jesus' words 'I am the good Shepherd' open out into a whole inner feeling experience, which is then unfolded in the rest of the chapter (John 10) or, 'I am the vine, you are the branches' (John 15). In this middle period of the Easter days we can try to make real these parables in our own behaviour. In Europe we can look at the work of shepherd and vine-dresser. Towards the end of this festival period, in the third third, we can try to rise from picture through parable to the spiritual reality of the Word. Christ speaks of his relationship to the Father and to the Spirit in beautiful, inspired words in Chapters 14 to 17 of the Gospel according to John. He speaks of their coming to dwell with the human being. The spirit of Easter leading to Ascension and then soon to Whitsun is a favourable time for an inner deepening of these words as real inner entities.

Throughout this festival we can try to remember Christ's words 'when two or three are gathered' (Matt. 18:20) and 'see, the kingdom of heaven is amongst you' (Luke 17:21, author's rendering), and not think we can realize Easter on our own. It is a sharing festival, and lends its sharing foundations to all other festivals. That is why Easter must be celebrated on the same day the world over and not be changed to a spring festival and celebrated seasonally—its primary experience is in sharing, not in dividing.

Summary

In the section 'Creating your festival' (p. 64) it was suggested one should look at Easter in three phases. The end of the last phase is the Monday, Tuesday and Wednesday before Ascension Day, which is always the Thursday of the sixth week of Easter. One may review during these three days what is experienced, built up and stored in the three phases (event, picture and word) and may oneself be ready to let it all be given up or sacrificed—given away to make space for what is to come. At the same time one can begin to revise the descriptions of the ascension—from the endings of the Gospel and the beginning of the Acts of the Apostles.

Afterword: Christ and Nature

The Easter account, in its widest sense, can show that new energy is carried into each of the realms of the natural fabric of the Earth and its kingdoms, and this energy is given a new pulse each year through celebrating these festivals.

The body of Christ has been laid out in a space hollowed in rock. There its mystery transubstantiation into the risen body affects the solid kingdom or earth element. The particles of fragments of the earthly, especially when it is moist as that limestone would have been, receive an impulse towards dissolving—in the opposite direction to that evolution which over aeons has hardened it. This is not dissolving in water but rather a loosening, and able, we could say now, all the better to be cultivated into life-supporting, living ground. And the elemental beings or nature spirits of this realm in their role as seed-quickeners start to be able to apply resurrection to the earth element itself. Earth acquires seed-quality: it will become something different in the future. This power is a life-power (or 'life ether'—an anthroposophical term designating a kind of counter-material in un-dimensioned or intensive space rather than the three-dimensional space in which our senses operate). It enables the earthly seed, which until germination is like a little stone, dead, to live and integrate into the whole life of the Earth. Life ether worked in nature before Christ, but Christ brought new resurrection life-ether which will in turn resurrect the Earth-body itself (when applied through human understanding and morality). This renews the destiny of the beings of the Earth (or 'gnomes').[18] They now not only help plants germinate or perform the other tasks they have but work to produce the new Earth with different mineral qualities from this one. The Book of Revelation describes the New Jerusalem with, amongst other mineral wonders, gold transparent as crystal (Rev. 21).

The Risen Christ is also seen by Mary Magdalene as the Gardener, or by the disciples as the one who knows where the water is full of fish. He is also the Lord of Life and of the watery realm of the Earth, culminating in his merging with cloud-nature at his ascension. His blood has penetrated the Earth and given its waters a new potential also, imbuing them with powers of regeneration. Water 'became' wine at Cana of Galilee (John 2:9); the Samaritan woman learned of springs of water welling up (from within the human body) to life beyond time (eternity) (John 4:14); the New Jerusalem features the River of Life flowing from the throne of God down the middle of the street of the city (Rev. 22:2). As Life penetrates the earthly, so is this watery element permeated by Easter which begets harmonies, life form and orderly relationships. The archetype is the juice of the grape, a parable of the blood of Christ flowing through a human community and ordering its diversities harmoniously. One can picture a wholeness to the Earth's life in her youth. Now Christ renews this ether through his speaking: his tone or form ether gives to the 'old' tone ether (also called 'chemical' ether) the potential to lead the new life ether seeds into growth whilst restoring the whole biosphere to its integrity. In this way it is the Risen Christ who can supply what Man's whole ecological striving really needs for its success—an ordering, harmonizing, forming power to the whole realm of what lives.

The airy realm too is changed. Man is dependent on nature to metabolize his breath. He exhales the semi-poisonous carbon dioxide, which is in turn assimilated by plants—they build themselves with it—and then give off the oxygen that we need to breathe. After speaking the greeting of peace, the Risen Christ breathes on the disciples (John 20:22) and says 'receive the Holy Spirit'—or holy breath! His breath does not need nature to metabolize it, but rather does it give purity to nature herself. Peace in the soul is the right preparation for a change of breathing, and this gift of Christ can be received. (We see here what western spirituality can rightfully answer, when it has grasped this, to the practice of yoga breathing). Peace works on the breath rather than us doing breathing exercises to create peace. Christ said, 'My peace I give to you. Not as the world gives do I give to you' (John). Crowd panic affects the breath and causes an odour in the human aura that animals can detect and which makes *them* fearful or aggressive. The elemental spirits of the air receive a kind of fall when this happens, but a resurrection when Christ appears in their kingdom—in the blossoming of the Earth, of the child in its joys, in the aura of the bride and groom in their concupiscence or in the thriving of a community. We speak of a breath of new life and can imagine the potential for resurrection out of certain heavy aspects of life in this gift of the resurrection in the aery ether of light. Many have certainly experienced significant events being accompanied by unusual light phenomena in the atmosphere, or breath-region of the Earth.

We can now begin to appreciate warmth as a state of its own rather than just a condition of the other states—solid, liquid and gaseous—and as such it is very closely interwoven with the supersensible realms of life, soul and spirit, all of which react to 'physical' warmth but can also generate warmth in their own realm. Enthusiasm can be repellent or positively contagious, depending on its truth and depth, but when it is truly 'being possessed by God', as the word means, we see it as a case of soul warmth originating in our spirit or I. This creates. It changes society, life and the world. Warm feet result! Christ's greeting, his breath, were warm. His being, when he meets someone, warms their life—also their death. Love is a fire. Christ gave fire spirits—the nature beings of the realm of warming and cooling—the potential to be the companions of human beings in their intelligence, so that a true spirit-mission, as we see in many great world figures in our troubled times, can be successful against impossible odds (of greed, envy, selfhood, revenge, power lust, etc.). They help us reach the angel of the other person.

There is another aspect of the relation of Christ to nature. Light has the appearance of being physical but it is really invisible. The Light of the World, as Christ called the 'I' principle of the human being (John 8:12) is himself. It becomes visible in its colour through engaging with matter. Personalities are colourful—all of them when adequately perceived! Nature is colourful. We can see the working of light when we distinguish between the qualities of direct sunlight (warm light), blue sky (light light), cloud-reflected light (light of form or harmony relating to water) and earth- or tree-reflected light (living light). All these show the ether-aspects of light, as it were laid down by Christ the creator. But in the phenomenon of polarized light, however, due to reflection off a shiny natural surface, the inner structure of the ether carrying it is altered. And when the reflected light 'interferes' or interweaves with the main flow, as it can do off the sea or off snow or ice fields, a structure is created in which the light is brought into a special dynamic. It can then enhance one's unperceived intuitions to become pictures before the inner eye. Christ can speak to us through this means about the future results of our deeds or the destinies that are approaching. This is an aspect of Easter that is developing and is again independent of the season, i.e. is valid the world over, for in March or April, when the Sun is in Aries or Taurus, the Lord of Life or 'Etheric Christ' renews his life-deed for the world.

Easter is the festival in which all these realms receive a mighty new heartbeat, but we can then pay careful regard to them throughout the year. Each festival chapter of this book can be all the better transformed into fruitfulness in this regard.

8
ASCENSION

Forty Days after Easter, for Ten Days

Motif

Christ is *still* present, spanning Heaven and Earth, but in the *cloud*, beyond our power of seeing. He is omnipresent and his power helps those (of whatever religion) who are striving to bring their free *spirit* into play in their *earthly* life and alter it according to *universal* values, rather than *materialistic* ones, to make progress.

He 'ascended into heaven' (Apostles' Creed) but has kept his feet on the Earth.

Nature: the cloud

In the chapter on Advent we looked at the theme of the Second Coming and described something of the nature of clouds. We can now look at this further. Water vapour, rising by the warmth of earth beneath and accelerated by internal dynamics, fills out the cloud so that it towers up and at the top becomes dazzlingly bright (nimbus). The vapour then disappears from sight to reappear almost magically as ice, and before our eyes is the full beauty of the 'cloud'. All four elements have intermingled. Earth (in the form of dust), water, air and heat are poised weightlessly, the water droplets not falling, the whole a living and orderly ascending and descending. Below there fall darker layers of stratus and above, against all common sense, the cirrus veil spreads, to create the likeness of a plant, with roots, leafy stems and petals.

A later development can be rain, which falls, life-bestowing, upon the earth. This is especially so if the cloud has first spread out to an anvil form, when thundery rain ensues. The heat in the cloud has overloaded the upper, airy, ethereal regions, which then discharge violently in lightning—the 'voice of the gods'. An Aboriginal wisdom sees in the thunder-rain the seed of the Lightning Man, fructifying the earth. Even those around Jesus realized that God had spoken to him when they heard thunder on Palm Sunday (John 12:28–30). '(Some) said it thundered, others that an angel had spoken to him, but Jesus answered, "This voice has come for your sake not for mine"' (paraphrase). And what was it that was said in answer to Jesus' words 'Father, reveal your Name'? 'I have revealed it and will reveal it again.' (Author's renderings.) This 'Name' is the I AM, the universal Ego, which is in the process of bestowing its divine spark again, upon Man. The Son of Man is what we take into ourselves in our inner striving. It is depicted outwardly in the lightning coming out of the 'cloud' (Luke 17:24): 'For as the lightning flashes in one part of the sky and lights up the other, so will the Son of Man be in his day of revelation.' (Author's rendering.)

There are many other cloud types and combinations, but this group is the central archetype, the total metamorphosis of all of them. With its darker, weightier stratus, its buoyant watery cumulus, its airy cirrus and fiery seed-bearing thundercloud it is the plant of the atmosphere, the intermediary between sky and earth, the medium of disappearance and appearance of the Lightning Man, the giver of life to the Earth.

As an archetype with many variations, it is also a mobile picture of the life of the Earth through day, month and year. As plants have their seasons over the Earth, in which they best show forth their glory, so does the cloud. In the region that was the cradle of Christianity the cloud shows itself best at Ascensiontide. And where the festivals are celebrated, *Christ reveals himself best* at Ascension too, having completed his mission as God Man, leading Man into death, resurrecting him with life and then rising, to embrace the whole life of Heaven and of the whole Earth.

Being so tied in this way to a seasonal phenomenon we must however say that Ascension shows all the more how important it is to celebrate festivals at the right cosmic time rather than the earthly seasonal one. For wherever Ascension is properly celebrated, those vital forces will be released into the life-realm of the locality to give it strength of earth, uplift of water, dynamics of air, then fire and renewal. We must here help nature spiritually, in an orderly way, to reveal the Lord of Life—a potency for the future rather than a dispensation of the past. Then Whitsun, that festival of human *unity* and *community*, can be built on new life and manifest as a common human aim towards freedom and responsibility.

Biblical context

The main account of this mysterious event is to be found in the New Testament at the beginning of the Acts of the Apostles (1:9), 'He was lifted up and a cloud received him out of their sight,' and includes a passage that has formed part of the theology of the 'Second Coming' (the expectation that Christ will one day appear again on the Earth): 'Why do you stand looking up into heaven? This Jesus who was taken up from you into heaven will come in the same way as you saw him go into heaven.' It connects to Jesus' own words (Luke 21:27): 'They will see the Son of Man coming in a cloud with power and great glory.' How are we to understand these words? The Apostles' Creed states, 'He ascended into heaven and sits at the right hand of God,' giving a succinct picture of departure from this world into the transcendent, matching the text of Mark's Gospel, 'He was taken up into heaven and sat down at the right hand of God' (Mark 16:19). Yet the Gospels included other aspects. In Luke it is only in *some* manuscripts that Jesus is carried up into heaven. The more common texts go no further than what must then be the main feature: 'lifting up his hands he blessed them. While he blessed them he departed from them. And they returned to Jerusalem with great joy.' (Luke 24:50.) Experience of the blessing must have far outshone that of the departure. Matthew describes nothing of these experiences but adds his own unique contribution at the very end of his Gospel, 'I am with you always, even to the end of the age.' This too speaks for Christ remaining connected with the Earth and humanity even though his full being has reattained its cosmic dimension.

Taken all together, the Gospels create a picture of Jesus entering a form of existence wider than that of his resurrected 'bodily' incarnation, which was a representation of a perfect, redeemed and raised humanity. As salt dissolves in water, its form vanishes but its substance becomes all-pervasive. This all-pervasive living element is called 'cloud'. The cloud does not dissolve earthly reality into nothingness so that suddenly Jesus can be in close proximity of the Father. No, Jesus permeates the cloud on his own initiative, just as he set in motion the final process of dying on his own initiative by breaking his body, the bread. As that sacramental deed is a blessing for all eternity on our bodily (fallen) nature so is this permeation of the cloud (biosphere), a blessing on our own vital (fallen) body, our life body or 'etheric' body.[19]

The disciples must have been shaken by this Ascension event. They spent the next ten days, until Pentecost (see next chapter), in a room in Jerusalem, working through their experience.

Thus far we are 'recipients of divine grace', in contrast to what comes later at Whitsun. That will be a spirit deed we must grasp in free initiative for it to be effective. In this light the picture of Jesus departing is seen as a warning of how things would be were he not to remain with us 'always', not only as resurrection but as life ('I am the resurrection and the life', John 11:25). The final 'historical' act of Ascensiontide is under Peter's initiative (Acts 1:15)—to fill the seat left empty after the betrayer had hanged himself. (One disciple had to fulfil the role of the Scorpion in the zodiac of the twelve apostles to enable Christ to redeem *all* human types). They debated the relative merits of possible candidates, put forward two, Barsabbas and Matthias, and then prayed for Christ to choose whom he wanted before drawing lots. Matthias was chosen.

Meditative pictures

1. Three related moments in the life of Jesus Christ, each on a hill—the transfiguration, the death on the cross and the ascension. How these are connected can be a theme for meditation.
2. What is the true nature of life and reproduction? Are traits really inherited or are they rather copied as one copies a model? Can one look at a plant and meditate away the material clothing until the individual plant is seen as an entity whose parts appear in related but metamorphosed forms according to their position on the plant: metamorphosis of 'leaf', the fundamental figure of the world of life. (We shall meet this picture again in enhanced form at Whitsun.)
3. The cloud is a manifold entity, a complex interaction of water, air, heat and particles of solid matter. In addition to the fourfold cloud, water itself can exist in states of ice, vapour or as a warmth dynamic sublimated beyond the vaporous, at the frontiers of matter—a warmth quality like that of a maturing compost heap rather than a burning fire. In clouds, water is constantly moving to and fro between these states, sublimely* making itself a symbol of the resurrected life that had informed the resurrection body of Jesus, now at Ascension free from its physical counterpart, free to move (and send life-giving 'rain' to) anywhere on the Earth.

* Sublimation: the property of ice to evaporate without melting, here extended to the next state-change, to become pure heat or 'quality' without being material. Sublime: a quality of transcendence.

4. A bud of, say, a rose, forms on the stem above the foliage, but only when all the leaves proper have finished developing and life-activity comes to a halt. The new life of the disciples that had *expanded* in the 39 days of Easter is now *contracted* to the 'upper room', from which the flower of Whitsun would come.
5. The cosmologies of many ancient cultures describe different ranks of spiritual beings. In a trinitarian one (as the Christian one is, which has given rise to this festival) they are grouped as three times three in a multi-dimensional image of the Godhead, with Man (Son of Man) below and God above. In the ten days of Ascension the resurrected Son of Man ascends through all these to reach the Godhead but *without* leaving Man and Earth behind, even if disappearing from view. He stands as a celebration of Man and God, expressed in his words quoted by Matthew (28:18): 'All authority in heaven and earth has been given me.' Since then he appears as the moving power of the cosmos and belongs to the totality of the Earth, planets, stars and beyond, being their Author.

Prayer

The account in Luke already mentioned (21:36), says, 'pray for strength to escape what is about to happen' (to the Earth and its inhabitants in terms of wars and destruction).

'Our Father—deliver us from evil' (Matt. 6:9) can also be our prayer, once we have focused on specific aspects of these themes.

Another prayer at this festival is that of the disciples mentioned at the beginning of this chapter—for the choice of their brother to be. It is a prayer for divine guidance in the final choice after they had gone as far as they could out of their own abilities and judgement. Have we lost anyone or do we need anyone in our life or work? Is that a gap for an unknown person to fill which would enable all of us to move forward?

Contemplation of nature—in northern and southern continents

Certainly in Europe the cirrus cap often appears for the first time in the year about now and demonstrates that the clouds have more vitality and tend to make form and metamorphose more than during winter and early spring. The new life of spring has risen from ground level to the sky. Trees have produced their first foliage, which will soon become darker and a strong background for the new shoots—which make some trees, especially the green and copper beeches, so beautiful around midsummer.

Bees are near the height of their activity. They too can rise to disappear in a 'cloud', swarming to take new life to another part of the Earth.

In the south the seasons are so different from the north—even in a locality where there is a similar set of seasons to Europe, that the above is not really unique to any particular time of the year. As Ascension is a festival for power to die at one locality in order to be available elsewhere, the tree and hedge phenomenon mentioned above can be seen as an Ascension quality whenever in the year these seasons occur.

Whichever hemisphere one inhabits, a part of oneself can well allow itself to ascend to a certain freedom from the weight of life, without lifting off too far. One's health may need attention; and the attitude that one's life is *on* the Earth *for* the Earth and its inhabitants is a sound one to foster. In some regions one has the challenge of sending power to others. In others, one is challenged to notice what is being bestowed as blessing from somewhere else and to cultivate the inner grace and capacity of will to receive it and render it effective.

The real nature contemplations for one's own locality are those one might see by looking at the clouds or watching the development of buds; then one can project the festival perspective onto the natural, 'etheric' one.[20]

Elemental interlude: the sylph

The cirrus clouds are flying high, their tails of icy hair rising higher still. The thin horizontal strands show the direction of the wind and the vertical ones the upward rising of thermal currents.

A flock of birds swoops by, swiftly determined to go their way, yet breathing in and out as they do so, swelling and contracting, especially to make a turn. Suddenly, we see how they accelerate upwards, as though flying up a waterfall. We can imagine that they are following an invisible path between two moving layers of air of different temperatures. Another time we see a flock of seagulls circling, drifting, rising up and gliding down. It is as though they are following the spirals around a large, nonsubstantial fir cone, with inner layers of differentiated warmth, always moving, always flowing.

It is another world up there. There is no need of earth to stand upon, for if we ourselves are made of warmth it is easy to glide across these layers of differentiated warmth. But we are heavy people, so we need paragliding equipment to do this. Someone described watching a large number of competing paragliders floating like this on the thermals and then noticing at the very top, high above the rest, a solitary eagle—the supreme of them all.

Every moving bird creates eddies in the air and it is they that support its weight. An eddy creates a lower pressure in the centre which draws into the airy element its supersensible counterpart, the light. But this is invisible light, as all true light really is. Otherwise we simply see illuminated material objects, not the light itself. If you can imagine a wake of such eddies following every bird and remember that you are in a weightless world, you might also imagine a sound that goes with it, a sound made up of all those tiny ripples and vibrations and audible only to special ears, perhaps birds' ears. Do not those small movements transmit the toning of loftier worlds? And between this invisible light and inaudible sound fly the sylphs.

Did you ever, as a child, want to be someone else? Did this wanting possess you, so that, knowing you could not be the other person, you hovered in their wake instead? This is how the sylphs feel when following birds. And as their longing builds up, they distil the tones of the upper heavens into song so that when the bird comes to rest it is able to make them physical and audible, as through an aura of light, colour, movement and an inexhaustible yearning joy. Sylphs can also lead birds to find a good nesting place, for they are the spiritual 'embodiment' of the bird's instinct, incorporated in its bodily form and structure.

In the realm of the plants, they weave light into leaf forms, knowing exactly which form belongs where on the stem, then focus it down into a thought-atom that is taken up by the undines we met in the Easter chapter and turned into substance—nature's alchemy or photosynthesis. Science describes what happens; the inner side of that, and its processes, is the doing of these elemental beings. Sylphs also remember what they have helped bring about; or better, they re-perceive it at the right moment. This is when the seed of that plant, which itself has no plant form, falls to earth. The sylph lets seep down into the earth the form of the plant so that when germination occurs, the image is there to inform its development. The sylph gives the earth its female forming power to bear, which is then quickened into life by the fire hidden in the seed. This idea of fire with the seed will be developed further in the chapter on St John's Tide.

Looking again at the high wisps of cloud in the healthy days of summer and at the birds flying on the warm air, we slowly divine that we are gazing at an archetype of the dream of nature's elemental spirituality that begets for us the song of bird and the beauty of blossom.

Creating your festival

1. Go into your room and place on a raised area some flowers, if possible with the leaves below and a single bud above. Study the expanding foliage halfway up and notice how the leaves become smaller and simpler towards the top and how a bud is lifted up by the stem. One bud can lead to many seeds just as the power of the Ascension can support the lives of many people.
2. Ascend a hill, noting the feeling when halfway up and then at the top with the world left behind below; see how one's mind and soul can work differently, more openly. Back down again, remember any new thoughts, ideas and intentions from one's ascent.
3. Look up to the clouds. Follow one patch in its movement. Try to draw it. Watch out especially for towering, ascending cumulus clouds to see the thin veil of the top detach itself gracefully, if there is a wind, or the cloud grow up through it. Here there is a chance to witness the change of state of water through vapour to ice crystals, and one can know that heat has been released into a world unseen. Sometimes these ice crystals engender the most beautiful colours, starting with pink and green, strengthening to yellow and blue and even a magical red.
4. Try and have a conversation with someone about the future care of the Earth environmentally and regarding the plight of those who are homeless.

Summary

Closing this festival is described in the next chapter; Ascension runs for ten days and passes over into Whitsun.

9
WHITSUN

Fifty Days after Easter

Motif

Pentecost—the fiftieth day—was a Jewish festival recalling the Jubilee year that adjusted 49 lunar years to 49 solar ones, so about 20 months. It was a time of restoration and reconciliation. The one-day festival of Pentecost (50 days after Passover) looked to the reconciliation of Israel through the return of Elijah to herald the Messiah. On this day, Fire visited the disciples—not that of Elijah but of the Holy Spirit—and gave birth to the Christian church. This force can also visit human life today.

Maturity alone is not sufficient to carry out a resolve. Drive is needed—but also a place of operation where this drive can be applied! For *human* affairs this must be a 'place' amongst human beings: the human place, community or 'abode'. I want to use this word to highlight a connection with the Gospel text that suits this festival (John 14), where the phrase comes, 'Whoever truly loves me, reveals my spirit; and my Father will love him and we shall come to him and make our *abode* with him.' Whitsun is not the festival of, say, a philosopher or inventor pondering until enlightened, but the enlightenment and enthusiasm that comes when members of a community (at least 'two or three', Matt. 18:20) struggle to work together for a common aim—one that goes beyond personal or national interests to the level of humanity as such. This is the festival in which that power can be released that can heal international strife, not by means of outer force but through the union of different peoples by a vision greater than all, giving them mutual understanding, cooperative toleration and a common goal for which to strive together.

The spirit of Whitsun bestows understanding, warmth of will and an eye for opportunity. It is the festival of a freedom in which these things carry the stamp of *personality*. In earlier times the right outer form sufficed for inspiration and success, for example a tribal council of elders, a ritual, a festival of peace, war, fertility or hunting. It could work like magic. This is not now adequate. The right forms are now those which mediate between individuals' responsibilities and free initiatives so these may be shared and responded to by everyone in the group, perhaps involving the sacrifice of one's own aims through insight into those of others and offering assistance to help others to contribute to the whole. In this way the members of the group gradually find their own places and roles for the whole. The new forms arise now through the interaction of *personalities* with each other and with the common goal. They promote greater freedom and greater character building and responsibility than in former times.

Whitsun stands in the year at the end of the second cycle of festivals, following directly upon Ascension, and at the beginning of the third (see Chapter 1). It can thereby be seen as that part of the work of Christ which blossoms into the Spirit and the future. Christ sends the Spirit to people on Earth. The third cycle is that of the Spirit *in its own realm*. From this point of view, Whitsun is at the beginning, i.e. the aspect of the Spirit of the *Father*. The Spirit is the spirit of new impulses; the Father gives them substance out of himself at Pentecost. The disciples found the Spirit as a new ground on which to stand. Where the Spirit works today, the new forms mentioned above also provide a ground for support and orientation. But as the annual festivals make a cycle, these forms can evolve year by year. From this ground- or Father-aspect of the Spirit, a new community such as mentioned here will go through a crisis of cohesion. The school, farm, team, research project, whatever it is, will be threatened with disintegration but the Whitsun qualities within it will see it through death into resurrection. From there on it has won its place in the world. The twelve and the one is a form of community that appears in many cultures and religions from the sons of Israel through covens and the Round Table to the college of Bodhisattvas and twelve pairs of Elders in the Book of Revelation. Now, through the potential of Christianity in its bridging between the material, earthly aspect of life and the ideal, spiritual one, the Whitsun spirit can be a powerful orientation in our battle with the divisive threat of a merely intellectual assessment of life's tasks and problems.

Nature

In its bud, at the peak of the leafy growth, the plant gave, as we saw in the previous chapter, a picture of Ascension. Now the bud opens. In Europe many trees start to form seeds (as also the dandelions!), but seed forming is hardly localized in any part of the year—in the Holy Land it was the time of the barley harvest, the first harvest of the year.

Most countries know the phenomenon of *something* seeding at any time of the year, so this festival touches nature everywhere at once with the same gesture: we receive seed from her to eat and to sow. Likewise with our own human genius. Our creative deeds feed ourselves and each other and we must not forget the Earth. We too must find ways to propagate our seed: for wind our words, for birds our thoughts, for gravity our own moral weight.

Biblical context

The Whitsun event is described in Chapter 2 of the Acts of the Apostles, directly after the Ascension narrative. The scene is set first by the reconstitution of the circle of the Twelve through the calling of Matthias to replace Judas Iscariot and then by the Jewish preparation for the festival of Pentecost, the fiftieth day after Passover. One of the features of this festival was a dawn watch for the coming of Elijah to prepare the way for the Messiah. Elijah had been taken up to heaven in a whirlwind (2 Kings 2:11) but the disciples had been told by Jesus that Elijah had already come, as John the Baptist, and they themselves had acknowledged Jesus Christ as the Messiah (*Messiah*, Hebrew = *Christ*, Greek = the anointed one). So the disciples would not now quite have known what to expect, what to look for on this special day. Then came, instead of the fire of Elijah's chariot, the wind of the Spirit (see John 3:8) and the tongues of fire of the Spirit, giving the disciples both a deeper intuition of the mysteries taught them by Jesus (John 14:26), and a powerful impulse of language enabling them to communicate and heal in a new way. Tradition then has it that as each spoke out his own individual inspiration, the Apostles' Creed was born. Peter preached and later that day 3000 were baptized: the church was born.

Meditative pictures

1. The circle of the twelve, with a wise Mother of Jesus in their midst as focus for her heavenly counterpart and guide, the Holy

Spirit. She weaves amongst the twelve starry constellations for the future of humanity (cf. the idea that the Twelve Disciples represent the twelve signs of the zodiac).

2. A dandelion flower bud opens to the light, receives the driving warmth of pollen. Then seeds mature, to fly far away for a new—deep-rooted—plant to be sown in the earth, one that can crack rocks and push through all life's obstacles.
3. Joseph the father, the devout Jew, who innocently begets the Son of Man upon the Maiden Mother, the immaculate, unconscious conception, with the impregnating male fire not of the Folk Spirit of the Hebrew peoples—as a devout Jew would hope—but of the spirit of humanity itself, the Holy Spirit (Matt. 1:20).
4. Here is something really worth spending half an hour at a time over several days—to achieve a new way of perceiving things. Use a simple annual flowering plant as an object of observation. Look at and study the different forms of leaf, sepal, petal and their intermediary stages up the stem. One can be amazed at the infinite variety of the sensitive minor variations. Then picture each form in the sequence of its occurrence up the plant stem. (Try this out before reading further . . .). Refer to the original plant until you can remember the forms, then in meditation run the series forwards and backwards (up and down the stem). Then let the bud open and do the same with the organs of the flower: sepal, petal, stamen and stigma. Finally study the development of the ovary and seed in the same way. Join all in one great metamorphosis, from old seed to new. There are those who try this and there are those just content to know about it.

From the visible Forms we derive a sensation of the steps *between* them which are really *not* seen: the movement or metamorphosis. At last, in grasping the metamorphosis of the whole plant we have an inner, spiritual picture of that which is the *gesture* of the metamorphosis, the gesture of the plant as a whole. We now *know* how the plant produces upon us the gesture and impression that it does. This is a real, methodically acquired, intuition of the being of the plant. It is a being with a living form, invisible, in constant flux, whose outer garment, which hides it yet at once manifests it, is made of carbon, oxygen, hydrogen, sulphur and iron!

Such a meditation will show us, in the way it is constructed, something that can be done for many other things, revealing their secrets. And as we have used the plant as an illustration of the festivals of this cycle, its meditation may thus reveal something of their secrets too.

Prayer

Appropriate for Whitsun are prayers for the whole world, for harmony and cooperation between peoples, for human rights, for the voice of conscience to be heard, indeed even to be spoken. Bodies which carry the destinies of the world's peoples also need prayers to find the forms and insights which enable individual and community to serve each other in a free way (for example governments, religious leaders, scientists).

Contemplation of nature—in northern and southern continents

Whitsun hardly has the connection to nature that one is accustomed to feel with other festivals and therefore can be considered for the *whole Earth,* and is a step to freeing the Christian festivals from nature in order to be able to give them back to her. The challenge with Whitsun-nature is to see the truth behind the glory. What is nature really? Earlier views of the world saw her as the veil of active spiritual beings who guided and nourished humanity and for their part required human knowledge for their own sustenance, whether in the form of ideas or sacrifices. Today we have the chance of using our freedom in knowledge to work beyond the materialistic view of nature, just as a forensic scientist construes a real, living being from the threads of his garments. For method we can learn much from the nature studies of Johann von Goethe, D'Arcy Thompson and others; these were taken up to a higher level by Rudolf Steiner, who included for the first time comprehensive accounts of the beings active in nature. More important in our studies, however, is to see that nature, though an earthly support of human life and to some degree culture, is not the *bestower* of spirituality but a needy *recipient* of it, ever since the first Whit Sunday. Paul saw this in his remarking to the Romans that nature needed man's help to release her from her travail (Rom. 8:19–22: '. . . creation itself will be released from its bondage to decay and achieve the liberty enjoyed by the Sons of God . . .'); this, even though he was indeed not a participant of Whitsun but one who had had his own Whitsun experience later.

Whoever has insight into this will not want to make the *season* in which a festival occurs in the *Northern* Hemisphere the dominant factor of a *festival* in the Southern Hemisphere. They will want, in the spirit of Whitsun, to keep the whole of mankind united in celebrating what is needed to renew the Earth itself.

Creating your festival

Clear away any outer signs of Ascension, and on the Saturday evening put out any items chosen for Whitsun. Is everything complete? Are there any gaps? By analogy with Acts 2, the Whitsun narrative, how shall 'Scorpion' forces (there in the figure of Judas) be replaced by something completely new (Matthias) to restore wholeness and wholesomeness? What can represent a figure of a wise Mother Widow as a focus for the form?

As a festival of freedom, freedom of our personal inner flame of spirit with which we feel at once individual *and* united with all others, freedom from our darker parts (because we have faced and worked with them through Lent and Easter), the approach to this festival must also be a *free* one. We are speaking of it as an adult festival (in contrast to a children's one, at which a certain repetition of imagery year by year is desirable) and one which can really bear the stamp of our inner person.

Imagine this person dwelling in a house with two windows, a table, a fireplace and the door. (On the table is something that represents the twelve and the one). We light a fire of all the remnants of the last seven weeks, then we look out through one window at the world and try to meet what comes in to us, what speaks to us, or wants to share our fire with deep feeling. We gather up an extract of it and put it around the centrepiece on our table and eat our meal. We digest with our meal what we have felt, then look out of the other window with thoughts that have arisen and try to see the path on which they want to lead us outwards. Then we put on our white mantle, take a last morsel from the table, fire from the hearth, open the door and stride forth. The world has asked, been heard, met our spirit, called us out. The spirit in Man works out of, for and with the Spirit of the World.

To initiate something on Whit Sunday can lead to a process that expands over a few days until it is established.

Summary

There are two existing festive days in the calendar which lend themselves well to adaptation as a rounding off of this linked group of festivals: Trinity Sunday, the Sunday after Whitsun; and Corpus Christi, the Thursday following that. Both are the more inward type of festival. What do we imagine under Trinity? Theology through the ages has struggled with the Three and the One, but what about the many triads connected with Man (created in God's image and therefore also a trinity)? Here is a festival chance to look at the following triads: creating, maintaining, destroying; body, soul, spirit; the elements of thinking, feeling and willing in the human being. Each has played a part in this chapter. They are each only alive when the other two are also active within them. It is one thing to think of a trinity in the abstract, another to see it working in creation.

Corpus Christi—eleven days after Whitsun

Corpus Christi is a festival of a quite different nature. It began in Liège in 1246 when Julienne, a prioress of Mont Cornillon, had a vision that this festival was needed to emphasize that the consecrated host really was the body of Christ. This was at once taken up by the church in Liège. It later became a festival for the whole church under Pope Urban when a celebrating priest, who had had doubts about the form in which this doctrine was taught by the church, experienced, after the transubstantiation, blood running from the host down into the marble of the altar.

In 1311 it became the principal festival of the church, with the consecrated host being processed through the streets, followed by mummers and mystery plays, somewhat as in ancient Egypt the gods were brought out of the temples and processed through streets and countryside with solemn festivity.

For Pope Urban, that priest's experience was proof of a doctrine concerning Christ's rather important words 'this is my body'. But for the Reformation such an experience just showed the superstition surrounding a 'magical' interpretation of them and the great festival was suppressed.

What of us today? A fitting ending to Whitsuntide, being a festival so deeply rooted in the events of the Last Supper at which those key words 'this is my body' were spoken, might be to turn the gaze of our new-found, free-thinking eye of thought and knowledge towards a mystery which for centuries the church had dogmatized for faith only. A science of weighing and measuring can do little with this mystery (which did indeed once need protecting from it). 'Transubstantiation' is a mystery that does at present transcend thought but has in it the power to raise thinking up to itself. It involves carrying something earthly, the living entities that wear the sense garments of bread and wine, that belong to the past, across into the future, beyond the threshold of death. If the cycle of festivals helps us grasp the Risen Man in time-cycles, so will a prayerful meditation on transubstantiation of bread and wine perceive him as Lord of the Elements—a body and blood not subject to time.

This is done by letting Christ's last days before death pass through our mind, then make the step into the resurrection narratives at the end of each Gospel. We find that this transition is the archetype of transubstantiation and so raises our mental capacity into its own eternal sphere. This will lead to a transcendence of the material brain and liberate our thinking capacity to embrace the spiritual. This time body really does embrace the cycle of the growth of corn and the making of bread, and the cultivation and harvesting of the fruit of the vine. By contemplating bread and wine, the body and blood of the Son, we can find the way from the Father-substance of nature to the Spirit-light of World-wisdom.

'Trans-substantiation' then comes into its own true meaning: to carry *substance* across (*trans-*) from the realm of nature to a new world—the 'second Creation' outlined in Chapter 1. This is what our festival impulse is about—preparation for that future evolution of mankind and the Earth that arises (resurrects) out of the old order through the co-working of God as Trinity and Man, in community.

10

ST JOHN'S TIDE

24 June, for One Month

This festival celebrates the birth of John the Baptist and describes how the fruits of our celebration of Whitsun can be developed further, along the path to Michaelmas.

Motif

First some background. Christianity is anchored in the cycle of the year at two points, Easter and Christmas. The keystone of this religion, Easter, with the resurrection, is a development and fulfilment of the Jewish Passover (see chapter on 'Easter'), inaugurated in northern Egypt at the time of Moses (*c.* 13 BC). It occasioned a new calendar-reckoning for the Israelites (Exod. 12:2) and was subsequently celebrated as a commemoration, in the first month, marked by the new moon following the spring equinox. It therefore has no connection with our spring. There would be lambs available throughout the year, so this is not a major festival based on a religious custom of the land. It is a festival brought into the order of the year, by divine intervention, during the time when, through the precession of the equinoxes, the Sun was moving out of the sign of Taurus—the whole inspirer of Egyptian religion at the time—into Aries, the Ram. The ram god Amun was dominant at that time and had certain traits comparable to that of Jehovah in the spiritual guidance of the people. The difference, however, was that Jehovah worked into the elements of nature from beyond, from the spiritual realms proper, whilst Amun had risen up from realms of nature, from the ranks of a nature or geographical deity. So the Egyptians at the time of the first Passover were fundamentally of a different spiritual disposition to the 'progressive' Jehovah-orientated Moses.

As remarked in the chapter on Easter, Passover is an emancipation from a religion grounded in nature-phenomena in favour of the needs of the evolving human soul, and Easter is a festival of the same gesture but now within us: the emancipation from the powers of death which originate in the fallen bodily nature and threaten to drag the soul down into the 'second death' (Rev. 20:6). (Note: It is not the body which 'originated' the Fall but the soul; the body, however, is marked by it and transmits it, hence the phrases 'original sin', 'inherited sin'.)

In Jerusalem, the Passover could have taken on a great connection with nature, through the observation of the New Moon two weeks before, to mark the New Year, but did not. Only in our Easter has this happened. The grave, and therefore the resurrection, was in a garden, but the resurrected Jesus did not appear as a god of nature but as a gardener (John 20:15) — someone who studies nature in order to re-form her out of their own inner, spiritual abilities from her own potential to be bountiful and ever create surpluses. Modern Easter *as a celebration of spring* has taken a questionable turn. We should not be celebrating that which nature produces, springlike, out of herself, but what man produces out of his enlightened husbandry. One can see here scope for those regions where April is autumnal, harvesty. For nature in herself it is the element of light which *can* be followed, for the sunlight flowing from Aries (in April) has its own celebratory quality of rebirth wherever on Earth it physically falls. This 'research' is in fact hindered if one remains in one place on the Earth, for then one sees light only in relationship to what is happening in landscape and growth. One would need to know the metamorphosis of light through the year at several latitudes to be able to extract its cosmic/stellar qualities and gestures. This needs to be borne in mind when we now arrive at contemplation of nature at *St John's Tide.* At Easter a divinely permeated and transubstantiated human being gave new impulse to both human and natural life. Since the first Whitsun and its yearly renewal, human beings can find their life path together enthused and enlightened from *within.* Now, at St John's Tide, is added a *cosmic* light, the light which, in flowing from the sign of Cancer (not the *constellation* of the Crab, but the region between Bull and Twins as a consequence of the precession of the equinoxes mentioned earlier) is focused by the Sun, mingled with creative life and set free in the aura of the Earth—the *whole* Earth. The Earth's aura, itself borne by breathing beings of fire and light, responds—with a different weaving in north and south. There is no harm in having 'Christmas' dinner in June on the snowy peaks of the Great Dividing Range but one is putting a knot in the etheric flow within the Earth's aura if one there introduces a festival of that other root of Christianity, the birth of the Christ child.

Jehovah, with the Christ approaching Earth and birth shining within him, overtook Amun as God of the chosen people and, as the pillar of cloud and fire, led them out of Egypt. Jehovah, in his role as director of conception—a role amply illustrated in the Old Testament as noted in our Advent chapter—has, with Jesus, handed over his task to the Spirit of all humanity: 'conceived by the Holy Spirit' (Apostles' Creed). The chosen people is now the whole of mankind, and the Christ child is to be born into humanity once only in history and once only in history's essence in the cycle of festivals within each year.

Jehovah's other role as folk-guide has also been handed on. Elijah stood before him (1 Kings 17) and guided the Israelites on his behalf, his mantle bearing in it the vital forces of nature (illustrated in Elijah's deeds with rain, fire, foodstuffs and life). John the Baptist, whose birthday is here being remembered, is to be a bearer of the Holy Spirit from conception (Luke 1:17) and will live in the spirit and power of Elijah. Since his death this mantle has expanded, first to embrace the Twelve and depicted most wonderfully in the Feeding of the Five Thousand (John 6), a great metamorphosis of the miracle of Elijah and the widow of Zarephath (1 Kings 17) now with Christ at its centre with the Twelve around him, and clearly showing that through him all the twelve signs of the starry zodiac have had their light focused into the bread that he blessed, broke and shared. This happened just before Passover, the year before the Last Supper. When today bread is consecrated, whether by ritual, by high spiritual faculties or by loving hearts and hands, it is truly an emancipation from racial as well as geographical deities into the truly universal, divine human. This mantle of Elijah-John is now the elemental mantle of the Earth, woven from the starlight *descending*, the powers of nature *revolving* and the Christian festival-light *colouring* from human hearts inspired by what the 'beloved disciple' must have heard, leaning on the breast of Christ at the Last Supper when he broke the bread (John 13:23). It clothes the bread in a new aura, in parallel to the new Substance invading it in response to the prayer. When the consecration is carried out by a human ego striving to allow permeation by the resurrected divine Ego, we can say, 'I am the Bread of Life' (John 6:35).

We can focus this at St John's Tide. We can see nature represented by the Father now supporting us with substance as a Mother, while the Spirit of the Universe rays down in conception, now as Father, begetter; and on the Earth's surface stands John, baptizing. Jesus thereby became Christ, and Man became his brother. In our time the spirit of John is that which witnesses what the light is doing in man and nature. To be full human beings we need to find our way into grasping this. This means observing the quality of the light at midsummer, as it shines in east, west, north and south, with artistic eyes, and noticing the impression it creates within us as though shining into darkness. A 'southern' festival will do the same in a reversed space but not a reversed time. This is a research question. The author has no impression whatsoever of July in the Southern Hemisphere but knows that a St John festival based on the spiritual background described above will interweave harmoniously with the Earth-fabric of the mantle of mankind, the whole Earth over. Nature's light shines into and transforms nature's darkness; Spirit-light penetrates matter; human life takes a further step to transform nature-matter-Earth's life.

Nature

We are used to the idea that towards midsummer the days are getting longer: the Sun rises earlier and sets later. Then, at the solstice (21 June), we believe, this is reversed until the winter solstice. But it is more complicated than that. The earliest sunrise is a few days *before* the solstice and the latest *sunset* also. This means there are ten days or so *during which the days are almost exactly the same length but each day shifts a few seconds later, centred on 21 June*. So St John's Day is the longest evening and the earliest dawn is already past.

At night, look for light in the sky just after dark—pale veils of flowing light high in the atmosphere against the darkness. They seem to whisper in the fading warmth: these are 'noctilucent' clouds, i.e. those that shine at night. These accompany the 'holy days of summer', when very high clouds still catch the sunlight scattered by the atmosphere while the Sun is not that far below the horizon. In the south, the Sun is low in the sky, calling up an inner warmth. The sign of Cancer sends the same warmth but it works from below, within us. If it is winter where we are, where is that leap between the incurling spiral and the outcurling one of Cancer's symbol? It is in the seed in the earth, waiting to germinate.

Biblical context

The Jewish people expected the Messiah, or 'anointed one of God'—in Greek 'Christ'—to redeem their fallen nature, their loss of paradise and contact with it, and also to liberate them from the Roman yoke.

At the altar of incense in the temple, Zechariah the priest had a vision of

Gabriel, the archangel associated with birth, telling him that despite their advanced age he and his wife would have a son, and they must call him John (Luke 1:13). He would carry the spirit and power of Elijah, the Old Testament prophet who overcame King Ahab and his Phoenician wife Jezebel (they persecuted the prophets and established foreign worship) (1 Kings 18).

The birth of John was associated with midsummer and is now celebrated on 24 June, three days after the summer solstice. It forms a polarity with Christmas Eve, three days after the winter one. John's Sun-sign is therefore Cancer, a double spiral, inwards and outwards, with a space of transition from old to new in the centre. He later said of Jesus: 'He must increase, I must decrease' (John 3:13).

John grew to be John the Baptist. He baptized Jesus when both were about 30. The mothers were cousins (Luke 1:36) and the artist Raphael supported the tradition of the closeness of the boys in many beautiful and mysterious paintings.

The above-mentioned Crab symbol (♋)can be seen behind the 'jumps' or new evolutionary steps between the men John and Jesus and between Jesus and Christ, where there is a break in continuity, although the next step can be seen to belong to the earlier. It is just that the link is not logical but comes from another order of 'things'.

John is depicted as a hermit in contrast to the social Jesus. He is one of only two human beings with a major festival dedicated to him in the Christian cycle of the year, indicating that he has an eternal role in addition to the historical one, the other being Mary, at Candlemas.

John was finally beheaded by Herod (Mark 6:18), an echo of the conflict of Elijah with Ahab and Jezebel, after he denounced Herod's marriage to Herodias, previously married to one of his relatives, Philip.

Meditative pictures

The Gospel references that follow are well suited to the activity of making pictures before the mind's eye. This can then lead to 'picture meditation' if wished, where one concentrates for a while on the picture thus built, then makes the extra effort to erase it and concentrate for a while on the empty space left. This will deepen the experience of each scene. (Note: it is not intended that this must be done for every reference. One has to carry out one's daily responsibilities as well!)

1. The Voice. 'I am the Voice of one crying in the wilderness. Prepare ye the way of the Lord' (Mark 1:3). Whilst Elijah was able to control rain, food, breath and fire (1 Kings, 17:1–16), John did none of these things. These qualities from the Old Testament are concentrated into a Voice in the New. So concentrated was he on his mission to prepare for Christ (the Logos = *Word*) through the medium of the Word that of his own person he was aware of nothing. (John 1:23.)
2. 'I send my angel before thy face' (Mark 1:2)—God speaks to Christ before the Incarnation.
3. The feeding of the widow of Zarephath (1 Kings 17:1–16) and the feeding of the Five Thousand (John 6:4–13).
4. Matthew 11:14: 'If you are prepared to accept it he was Elijah who is to come.'
5. Luke 9:9: 'John I beheaded but who is this who performs such deeds?'
6. John 1:31: 'I myself did not know him but for this I came baptizing with water, that he should be revealed to Israel.'
7. John 1:33: 'He who sent me ... said, "He on whom you see the Spirit descend and remain, this is he who baptizes with the Holy Spirit."'
8. There are two paragraphs in John 3 where it is not obvious whether they are the words of Jesus or 'the beloved disciple' Lazarus, who wrote the Gospel: v16, 'For God so loved the world ...' and v31, 'He who comes from above is above all ...' Are they inspired by John the Baptist?
9. The disciple Lazarus, not of the Twelve, becomes known as John after being raised from the dead, and is at the centre of the scene of the Last Supper, leaning on the breast of Jesus. He is the evangelist with the most intimate accounts of John the Baptist.

Prayer

For people and situations, we can pray for new attitudes and ideas for the future. For redemption of the problems that beset humanity and the traits causing them, cultivate a prayer for the redemptive work of Christ that can follow self-knowledge and conscience—change in heart and tolerance of others. Pray that *warmth* of heart can rise into the mind for grasping universal *ideas*—and flow down into the hands and feet for *deeds* on life's path, that the fabric of the world also be changed. In this way we can realize John's exhortation 'Repent', i.e., 'Change the ways of your minds and hearts.' For in this way our deeds will have their power in our feelings for the world and be guided by our inspirations about it.

A prayer based on some of the motifs of John's Gospel:

The growing of corn lets light into the grain
The baking of bread lets life die, to rise again
The offering of bread lets love abide.
Let light become life
Let life become love
Let love feed
In giving and in taking
Union and Communion.

Contemplation of nature—in northern and southern continents

The author can only offer European experiences here. Make time to take a woodland walk one afternoon. See how the sunlight reaches down to the forest floor, leaving shining patches amongst the shadows. Note how these then become a light *source,* not just a reflection. They send light of a 'looser' constitution into the shady areas. This is to do with the fact that this shade is different from the individual shadows of an open landscape. They are 'penumbral', half-shadows which enable some of the more unusual colour and light phenomena to manifest and open the way to a really wide artistic grasp of light so that the statement 'I am the Light of the World' takes on a scientific, existential meaning as well as a theological and transcendent one, which develops further in August.

This is not only the Sun's high point; it is the peak of the honeybees' season. The brood is thriving, perhaps there is a surge of activity after swarming but there will be more swarms (casts) filling the air with that special joyous sound as they fly to and fro at high speed. Stand quietly in their midst if you have the chance. That is almost a feeling of the St John's Tide spirit. He after all lived partly off honey and must himself have known this experience. Bees are most good-natured during swarming, being full of honey for the journey to have substance to convert into wax for their new home.

Bee nature is laid, in continuous movement, over plant nature in a true marital fructification of Earth and spirit; for plants are Earth beings that express the life of the Earth (their blossoms are heavenly visitors as you can tell by looking at them in contrast to the leaves) and bees are of Heaven (they import some of it into their hive). Here, with a little imagination, we can imagine the bees representing the warmth forces of the 'Spirit Father' conceiving upon the water substance of the 'Mother of Matter' or 'Earth Mother'.[21] Visit a hive in the twilight and smell the nectar of the day's harvest expanding as the daylight slips slowly away. All this gives the background mood for the different themes of this chapter. May it lift our comprehension of them into a higher state than just the mental one.

Elemental interlude

Sitting gazing into the fire in the grate many impressions home in to my soul.

I see moving colour, warm colour—reds and yellows. The movement never stops. The fire is all movement.

I feel the warmth. The warmth too is moving, now hotter, now less hot. The skin on my face sees the warmth as my eyes see the flickering colour.

And my soul sees them both too; and somehow the fire belongs in my soul: it is at home there. And my soul is at home in the fire.

I also see darkness. There is darkness as a shadow beneath the wood of the fire but when the fire flashes brightly, shadows are scattered about the room. They move. My soul is alive to the lights and the shadows.

When the fire is young, newly lit, its movement, and its lights and shadows, are lively. As it grows older it becomes steadier, constant. But then I can see the flames better. If you look at a gas flame, you will see it as a kind of bud shape with blue in the middle of the yellow; but the flames of a fire are not like that. If you make the comparison, it looks as though a gas flame has been pushed in from above, so that the tongues of flame appear to be licking round something that is itself round—but not really there. Something dark within the orange flame.

What is it that presses in like this, as though visiting from another dimension? If we believe our eyes, they tell us that it is the 'negative' of heat. It is called in anthroposophy the warmth ether and works inwards in the opposite direction to the rising heat. In this way we can experience heat as on the one hand material, the burning carbon, and on the other etheric, a heat that is not carried by matter—no jostling molecules—but supersensible. We know this heat from our heart when it is warm towards something or somebody. It is an in-pressing heat, that ripens.

But we can also know it in our mind, in our thinking. Some ideas are cold—for example, that the universe has come about by chance or that the human being is only body and that our soul and spirit are illusory, just based on the electricity in our head. Other ideas are *warm*. Your baby really *is* the most special being in the universe and on this basis your parental sense really does sometimes know better than some 'authorities'.

One of the traditional names for those soul beings that live in the etheric medium of heat is 'salamander'. Perhaps you have seen one of these lizard-like creatures, black and yellow and rather slow in movement. They would of course creep out of a pile of logs in the woods if you set it alight and thereby they would represent the opposite movement to the shapes that we found in the fireplace in those dark spaces that the flames embrace. Their slowness would represent a contrast to the movement that we saw before. However, apart from that they contribute little to our imagination if we would wish to envisage the elemental being that we are talking about here. You would have to imagine larger and smaller salamanders. The larger one would be like a human being, rather more male than female and made out of heat. Within the movement you would perceive a being that wanted to relate to you and help you in the following ways. First, in situations where there are human difficulties. Here your salamander companion would help you find a warm word to say. He would find this by connecting your own self of the moment with your higher self which is always warm. In this role he serves the higher beings that try to teach love to the human being. A second situation is when you are lacking the right idea for something, whether mathematical or outwardly practical. Here the salamander can connect you with an intuition that is lodged somewhere in the darkness within your (spiritual) legs and make it light up in you and fire you with enthusiasm and energy for carrying it out. He is therefore in imagination the same size as you are but with a different countenance.

The smaller salamander is the one you will find outside in the garden or in the meadow. There they are really tiny and they create little power vehicles of warmth which carry pollen from one plant to another. A kind of plant heat has entered the pollen as it develops within the flower. The etheric counterpart of this heat is the tiny salamander that then carries it where it needs to go, somewhat like a fiery sprite. Upon arrival it leaves the pollen on the surface of the stigma and continues down the style into the ovary where it quickens the plant into seed-bearing. A larger variety of salamander then works (in a comparable way) to ripen the seed and accompany it into the earth when it falls there. In so doing, it channels heat from the cosmos into the earth as the Sky Father impregnating the Earth Mother. You can translate some of this to the mystery of human fertilization and gain some insight into the conversation between Father Joseph and the angel when he hears that the child is conceived by the Holy Spirit.

Another place where fire spirits work is between man and animal or animal and plant: rider and horse, shepherd and dog, lion-tamer and lion, child and lamb, Diana and falcon, and bee and flower. All these relationships generate a life connection between the two beings. Into the warmth of that relationship, out of the formless ether an 'elementary' life form is drawn, ensouled with hitherto *elementary* soul-substance that is temporal, temporary—and 'elemental'. In this way these beings can be seen as the 'offspring' of others of a higher and enduring nature, beyond that of spontaneous creation and dissolving away again into cosmic substance. One exception to this is where a nature being or other situation of a 'life' nature that attracts an elemental being (including our thoughts and feelings) is *understood*, i.e. placed within context and purpose, by us. Then that being is liberated from its bond to that place and carries with it as it dissolves into the cosmic ether and soul world the good fruits of that moment of acknowledgement of its humble purpose. Such soul substance is gathered by the progressive spirit of the age to help mankind towards a wholesome destiny. The opposite can happen too if we let the situation down through dullness of soul and will.

There are also giant salamanders that appear in volcanic outbreaks and the like. If you are looking for them, remember that they represent the polar opposite of the material phenomenon, a movement in the opposite direction from the flames, yet still beings of heat.

Since the fire beings are, of all the elemental beings, nearest to the creative heart of the cosmos, their influence supports this redemptive human approach to the world of nature by helping us, when we try to kindle warmth in our 'knowing'. They are still too 'elemental' to be called beings of love, but they make available a warmth substance in which love can grow—grow outwards expansively to embrace what is about us. The Celtic appellation of Christ as Lord of the Elements takes on deeper significance when we feel him as indwelling all occasions of love.

Gazing deeply into a fire in the grate or a bonfire in the garden lets the soul find the kind of peace and warm, quiet sense of fun that open the way to finding the fire spirit.

Rudolf Steiner describes these things in their fullness in the places referred to in earlier chapters.

Creating your festival

Let us remind ourselves of our way of looking at the cycle of festivals as three, so that their inner feeling qualities can be brought together into a creative dynamic that stems from the Trinity of Father (origin, birth), Son (creator in death and resurrection) and Spirit (fruitfulness and making wholesome). In this scheme, St John's Tide is the aspect of death and resurrection in the realm of Spirit. This triad has been inaugurated by Whitsun, the coming of 'the Spirit of the Father', and will come into fruition at Michaelmas. St John's Tide is therefore a festival of inner creativity and of finding a new beginning where affairs of life have come to a standstill. The long period between St John's Tide and Michaelmas is then a time for developing the new seeds of heart and mind for bringing fruit into the world.

This motif of death and resurrection—the 'three-day process'—also throws light on the fact that this Christian festival (as also Christmas) begins three days after the solstice. Christianity moves on from nature through the principle of resurrection.

Fire festivals took place to celebrate the Sun. This needs to change in our time into the inner process described in this chapter. A picture that we can include as a reality in any festival display illustrates this: the candle. It burns down: wax gives itself to light, flame carries ash away, the Earth is spiritualized by human life, the more lived, the less left.

So we need to be quite free in forming this festival, but can remember the ingredients of the others: a table piece, some shared study or contemplation, and our own brand of 'repenting': where does our soul require a change of heart for its own good and that of others?

Summary

It is a matter of feeling how long this festival lasts. Maybe the first twelve days are special, both in themselves and as an opposite to Christmas. But one could well extend to Lammas at the beginning of August. See next chapter.

Did we make New Year resolutions? Look back on them now, and brings them up to date. Make mid-year agenda points rather than resolutions, asking what the themes in our life that need taking out for fresh air and exercise are. In this way they can, in the autumn, in time for the Michaelmas season, be made into seeds that have a power of germination within our life, our biography. They will not just die away as nature will do as winter draws near.

11
LAMMAS

The First Few Days in August

Motif

Lammas means 'Loafmas', the festival of the loaf baked from the very first cut corn of the harvest—green corn—not left stooked to harden off but immediately threshed, milled and baked. Why a loaf?

What we have gained in insight and moral substance through the St John festival may now be 'harvested green'; for it really needs the time until Michaelmas to become fully ripe before being taken into earthly or spiritual action. But as green corn, not yet mature, it may be made into 'soul bread' and offered in our heart as on a personal altar. We can ponder it and discover first its 'message' or ideal content, then the motivation it begins to produce in us. It is like a personal communion that can run parallel to an outer Eucharist.

In pre-Christian times the union of Heaven and Earth was under the auspices and control of divine beings, demigods—indeed, Heaven and Earth acted as beings in this drama. Man was at once servant, focus and purpose of this great festival, which although taking place at Lammas embraced the whole year.

In Christian times it can be human beings working together who inaugurate and carry through this union throughout the year, finding ways through which the spiritual beings—both sublime and elemental—of both Heaven and Earth may be encouraged and enabled to work.

It is important for Christianity to 'husband' the Earth so that she is given *new* life and fruitfulness rather than utilize her inherent substances and forces. As these are clearly on the wane and it is also clear that divine intervention is apparently withheld on the physical plane, we must assume that this husbandry must be exercised by human beings. This is an important difference between the Celtic approach to Earth's fecundity and the Christian one, where the spirit of a festival is to let flow the force of the resurrection (see Chapter 8 on Easter) *into* the Earth rather than just what human nature can manage on its own. For a child to grow well, the parent needs to pass on ever greater responsibilities down to it. So also the

Creator will pass on responsibility and initiative for creation to the epitome of creation: Man.

Nature

The origins of this Sun festival lie in ancient pre-Christian times: the union, or marriage, of Sun and Earth (in Celtic, Lug and Eire). This is a very simple cosmic image of an important step in evolution, for in times earlier still Sun and Earth were separated by first a volcanic and later a dense misty atmosphere (as both spiritual science and physical science agree). As these atmospheric conditions developed towards more contemporary ones, the Sun Father came out of the clouds and shone directly upon the gradually solidifying Earth Mother. Moses describes the rainbow at this time, and God's covenant with Noah: 'While the earth remains, seed-time and harvest, cold and heat, summer and winter, day and night, shall not cease. Be fruitful and multiply and fill the earth.' Mankind was to be the guardian of nature's rhythms and fertility.

The celebration of this cosmic process settled gradually on one of the four main Celtic 'quarter day' festivals—Lughnasadh, now 1 August. These Celtic festivals, which divide the year into four quarters, are the four great pivotal festivals of nature: Lughnasadh; Samhain (All Souls'); Imbolc (Candlemas); and Beltane (May Day). They fall approximately midway between the four major Christian festivals of Christmas, Easter, St John's Tide and Michaelmas.

Biblical context

Lammas has been presented as a modernizing of Celtic tradition, a Christening of the relationship between Heaven and Earth expressed in the human being and his image as harvest loaf. We shall now see how the specifically Christian tradition regarding bread is grounded in the Old and New Testaments. This can be deepened through meditation. Although the theme of the divine is also there, it is the *bread* that we are concentrating on for the present purpose.

1. 1 Kings 17:14–16. Elijah asks a widow for a drink and then something to eat.

She gives of her best and as long as Elijah is present in her house and she is feeding him, her jar of flour and oil are never empty.

2. Matthew 2 'When Jesus was born in Bethlehem . . .'
   Bethlehem means *house of bread*. The Virgin is his mother.
3. John 6 and Mark 8 The feeding of the 5000 with five loaves and two fish . . .
   The feeding of the 4000 with seven loaves and a little fish . . .
   The constellation of the Virgin—bread (she holds a sheaf of corn)—and that of the Fishes—oil—face one another in the heavens. Bread and fish are offered in thanksgiving and shared.
4. John 6:32–41 'I am the Bread of Life . . . that came down from heaven.
5. John 13 Bread and wine are offered in thanksgiving and shared in anticipation of Communion. Bread and wine become the substances that after the resurrection can carry divine body and blood on the Earth and into human beings.
6. John 19:34 Earth Communion. The crucifixion: blood flows into the Earth.
   The burial and earthquake: the body substance enters the Earth.

In sharing Communion in *substance* (i.e. through a Communion service), what has taken place outside us in a non-natural way on the altar is taken *into* the *nature* of our metabolism.

In sharing communion in *thought* (for example in meditation or shared discussion, where one enters with interest into the thoughts of the other and an exchange arises that takes all involved to a more all-embracing view), what Christ has performed in carrying something of *nature* over into something of *spirit* is taken into *our* spirit, and lets it grow.

This, as basis of our own offering of bread as ourself, puts us on the path to communion with others in our community (union of Communion). It connects, through the ceremony, our *thinking* with other people and our *will* with the Earth.

Any one of the above images makes a helpful background to celebrating Lammas but the meditation is deepened by taking them as a series, as a metamorphosis of pictures. (See 'Meditative pictures' in Chapter 9 on Whitsun.) We gradually grasp the gesture and thus the inner being of the Bread of Life.

Meditative pictures

1. The harvest of corn and the baking of the loaf represent the first child of the cosmic union of Sun and Earth. It symbolizes the substance of man himself, for man is also born out of Sun and Earth. Genesis describes the forming of the first human being out of Earth substances, then the breathing into him of the divine breath. We see here how what has come over from earlier cosmic rounds was till then still held in the Godhead. This is what transforms all subsequent evolution—our spiritual dimension or ego—and that sets out on the path to freedom, but must first pass through the Fall.

   The loaf is much more than a fruit of nature. It has been raised by human activity—it shows what the Earth can do through Man when he cares for her life, and it shows what she can do for him as staff of life. (I am using *Man* here in distinction to *nature,* rather than *human being,* a word which implies a connection to the earth (humus), which at this point we are working to overcome.)
2. Seen like this, the loaf becomes the substance of sacrifice. First it was human blood that was needed to feed the Earth for her fruitfulness. For example the Pharaoh of ancient Egypt might, in prehistoric, pre-dynastic times (3000 BC), be sacrificed to this end. Stravinsky's *Rite of Spring* concerns Siberian customs of sacrificing a maiden to fructify the Earth even until recent times—although the sacrifices were made to *prepare* for fruitfulness rather than make thanksgiving for it. As times moved on, first slaves then animals were sacrificed instead, until gradually the loaf itself could be offered to Earth and Heaven and eaten by the human beings living between them, between 'seed-time and harvest'. The transition from human to animal sacrifice is indicated in the biblical story of Abraham and Isaac (Gen. 22), the one from animal to plant by the Last Supper—Passover lamb to bread and wine. The Egyptian and Celtic mysteries (also the Greek, see

next paragraph) thus anticipate the coming of Christianity in ritual. A possible transition to a mineral sacrifice in the future may be sought in a clarity of thought that is 'crystalline', as clear and light-filled as a quartz crystal and able to illuminate our spiritual and festival experiences.

3. Noah planted a vineyard, reminding us that in other countries it was a different sacrificial substance that took a central place. Whilst bread is life raised up from the Earth's womb by the Sun, wine is drawn down from the Sun by the waters of the Earth, working from her depths through the deep taproot. Whilst in Celtic regions it was only the corn mysteries that developed, we see in ancient Greece both the corn (Demeter) and the vine (Dionysos) mysteries arise.

Prayer

I feel myself as a nature being. My body is happy to feel the Sun shine warmly upon it. I am happy to walk along firm ground amidst the waving corn, then amidst the stubble amongst the stooks of corn. I am happy to see bags of grain sitting in the barn and fresh bread on the table in the kitchen.

I see beyond the Sun to the creation of the universe and I see beyond the Earth to the substance poured out at the beginning of creation to enable the human being to emerge from the darkness, conceived by Heaven and Earth in substance, conceived by the divine beings of Heaven and Earth in spirit. I pray in thanksgiving to Heaven and Earth for mothering my being, my life and giving me sustenance. I pray to the Father in thanksgiving for my spiritual being, my possibility to exist, strive and develop. Then I pray to the Spirit for enlightening my mind to take in the whole world. Many people on this Earth are outside my mind; many people on this Earth are without spirit-awareness of their own true existence.

Between myself and this world is the community in which I live and work, which I support and which sustains me. I pray to the Christ, whose place as Son is between the Father and the Spirit, to help me find my rightful place in my community, to serve the destinies of those around me and to receive the destiny that is brought to me through them, that my community may be a place of mutual blessing.

Contemplation of nature—in northern and southern continents

The North

The foliage of trees is at its thickest—no longer fresh but solid. Below the woodland canopy it is shady—sometimes deeply so. Look for where light reaches the ground—as a penumbral half-light of dreamy soft quality that we noted at St John's Tide. Now this August light warms the insect whose wings carry the warm illumination into the dark corners of the woods and whose shimmer lets the illuminated leaves become more like an impressionistic painting than solid nature. Can we notice a development of these subtle qualities since St John's Tide? Can we smell the quiet tread of 'dying-and-becoming' weaving between light and shadow where the ants work?

Please ponder on what is meant here. You may need to be out in the woods in the right place at the right moment to understand what is being indicated.

Keep awake, imitate the light and penetrate the darkness of humanity so that there too the source of human soul-light can be established. In other words, wrestle inside yourself to discover who you are and where you want to go, and why . . .

The South

The daylight is increasing perceptively now but is still shining against the background of the starry constellations of Twins and Crab as in the north. We can try to emancipate ourselves from the prejudice that light starts at one point and rays out, ever losing power, into its surroundings. It does ray, but in the right conditions its source can move with it, bestowing radiant power to the objects it touches or the media through which it passes, as leaves in a shady wood shine out as light *sources* instead of just reflectors. Here nature is already working in the way *we* may wish to do and we can follow the light outwardly as it enters growth, but also as it enters into the local 'fall' of those plants which start to wilt or shed their leaves at this season. What is the particular relationship of these plants to the interaction of light and darkness? How do the colours of their bark, leaves and fruits change in the changing light? Does the light falling on the fallen leaves glitter or shimmer on them? Are there leaves newly on the trees through which the light shines or reflects, now with gentleness, now with dazzle? Many questions—but invitations to observe! The one quality of light reaching the Earth does so here in increasing strength, whereas in the north it is doing so in a decreasing one. This phenomenon could be taken as an illustration that we may have the same festival the world over but articulate it in an opposite way between hemispheres.

These questions are challenging for the south. What phenomena of light, air, cloud and weather are to be found there? What is growing or dying in the plant and animal kingdoms that can portray the marriage of Heaven and Earth and in its fruitfulness enable us to use it as a 'green' harvest loaf for our inner and outer offering?

Creating your festival

Alone or in company: a walk in a cornfield. What type of grain is it? Do we know all the types grown in our own area? What position is the ear? How are the grains carried within it? How do they smell, feel, taste? What colour are they?

Is there a harvest festival in your community? Can you ask a farmer for a sheaf? Try to borrow a scythe or a swap-hook to experience reaping, and hear that unique sound of the blade, sharpened by the spirit-will of the reaper's mind working through his arm muscles into the whetstone. You could then hear the sound of the scythe crisply severing the hollow cornstalks.

Can you feel the threefoldness, the trinity, of ceremonially preparing and baking some fresh corn, setting aside another part of the harvest to mature as the annual food supply and retaining a selection of seed for future sowing (celebrating past, present and future)?

We can express this triad by bringing a token of nature into the home as a festive focus, as long as it means something to us for our own life. Which of our current personal achievements can be used as it stands, fresh from our own 'nature'? Which of them needs to be kept for further maturation in the company of the Sun Spirit of humanness until ready to be given out into the world? And which needs to be held over until an opportune time when we ourselves, our community and the world itself are in the right constellation for them to be received in a beneficial way (i.e. as an impulse for something new)?

Summary

Lammas picks up some of the themes from St John's Tide and is itself nearly halfway towards the next festival, Michaelmas. At St John's Tide we celebrated dying and becoming; at Michaelmas we shall celebrate that in the dying of nature the spirit can be born. At Lammas we sacrifice—let die away—what we have achieved, to open the way for new life both of nature and spirit.

The traditional day for the blessing of beehives is 8 August. If one wishes to leave the bees enough honey for their winter without having to feed them sugar-syrup, then, apart from special crops like heather, this is the end of the honey harvest.

12
MICHAELMAS

29 September

Motif

Courage, perseverance, sociability, creativity and spiritual research are the guiding motifs for this festival.

In the church year 29 September is marked as the festival of 'Saint Michael and all Angels', which was inaugurated around the eighth century. In 492 this archangel appeared on Monte Gargano (the 'spur' on the east coast of southern Italy), to encourage the people to withstand enemy onslaught. In the Old Testament he stands behind the phrase 'the Angel of the Lord', where the context is of doing battle, e.g. Joshua meeting him before the Battle of Jericho (Josh. 5:13). His Hebrew name can be rendered as 'Who like God?'. We might ask ourselves: are we only animals with the *illusion* of freedom and eternal life or are we, as all old traditions insist, made 'like God' (see Psalm 8: 'a little less than God') right from the beginning? So the answer is ourself. How far do we experience anything in ourselves that is godlike? We need to gain an idea of what God is like; and we also have to have some idea of what *we* ourselves are like.

Nature

How do we bring nature into this festival of the spirit? Our leading thought has been that although Man is *of* nature, his task is to *grow beyond* her and help transform *her* beyond herself, for example through right cultivation and husbandry. So nature in this *festival* has to illustrate where this can happen. Floral decoration is of course a very basic way in which artistic skill takes nature beyond herself, but the inventive spirit may find other ways. Golden autumn leaves can, besides showing autumn, be a symbol of an inner fire, which could be illustrated in southern lands by any reddish leaves of new growth. One then looks into nature for the following:

signs of decay and new growth;
signs of harvest and what can be gathered in as fruit for us and for the Earth's future (this can also be something like timber for artefacts or sculpture);
signs of a message to us like changes in animal behaviour or climate;
and, most importantly, we can look for an 'open space' in nature where we can introduce a change for positive evolution—for example in the question of agricultural seed and its fertility and truth to type. Should we make seed production science-based or use our knowledge to improve stock strength so that seed fertility is raised to at least its pre-industrialization level, if not higher? There are many such areas now: forest management, habitats, animal health and breeding but also human health and education: how are they informed by the question 'who like God?'? This question can open up a different approach to life. Here are some examples in more detail.

A Michaelmas picture: deriving science from nature (please read slowly!)
There is a veil of early morning mist hiding the bright blue sky. It gently lifts and falls with otherwise unnoticeable changes in ground-coolness and the warming air after the cold night which has made it visible.

It is a clean white, yet where thin it moves the darkness of the distant woodland shadows to blue and makes a golden brown of the lighter shades of the sky above the horizon.

This vapour, though evanescent and in itself colourless, has the potential to change what has been otherwise merely light or dark. After the blanket blackness of the night, the daylight reveals colour. Then this watery thinness of vapour shifts the colours into a different display, where they come away and live freely rather than being 'stuck' on the objects. Colour comes away and teaches me that the veil of the sense world is not glued on forever but at times lifts, lives, and—opens. We can see this when the light is right and we stand in the right place. And, look! The blue and gold in the sky mingle to a light green, and in another place, where they are strong enough, we see in the space between ourself and them a glorious pink such as might belong only to hosts of Heaven. This pink and this green are also often present through ice clouds in the region of the Sun where they also give us a feeling of being allowed to see into nature's secrets. When they appear in autumn their glory can open our imagination to 'resurrection' in the dark of winter.

This magenta pink has no individual 'wavelength'. It is more a lack of the wavelength of green; it does not find a place in school spectroscopy but needs conditions similar, but opposite to, the production of green, by projecting through the prism a narrow band of opaque material instead of a narrow slit of 'light'. You can experiment by looking through a prism, or by squinting through your eyebrows, at a narrow strip of window for green, and a window bar for magenta.

To sum up: what can be learned from this for science is that green is not the only 'middle of the "spectrum"' (= something ghostly, unreal!) but magenta makes an equal claim, for we can make the bow of colour the other way round. This asks us then to look again at all hypotheses based on the seven-colour-spectrum and not burden it with being 'absolute', for it has its counterpart in magenta flanked by cyan blue and lemon yellow. See the development in the next section.

A second Michaelmas picture deriving knowledge from nature

The Full Moon rises red and slowly becomes yellow. Then it looks almost white as we view it through decreasing atmosphere as it rises higher and higher. These colours do not belong intrinsically to the Moon but they *appear* upon it when its whiteness is damped down by intervening matter. Some physics has it that blue light's wavelengths have been scattered by this matter, leaving behind the yellows, oranges and reds.

Blue sky goes black at night when there is no light, but the blue returns in the morning, except near the Sun, whose power overtakes this process and makes the sky white.

So to see yellow we need to *look at* the source of light, for blue on the other hand the light must *come in sideways.*[22] Again, some physics maintains that here the yellow waves are dispersed, to leave the blue behind. But if we take away these thoughts of waves and look again we see that violet, blue and cyan (a greenless pale blue) *appear* when darkness is lit up from the side in a non-empty space (sky, smoke or mist) and yellow, orange and red *appear* when a light surface or source is covered by the darkness of matter—even the clean clear 'matter' of the air. The sky when seen through the thin air of a mountain top is more violet, whereas lower down on a normal bright day it is pure pale blue. And the Sun changes from white to gold, then red between noonday brilliance and sunset.

(This may not be so easy to grasp at first reading. Just go slowly over it a few times and picture it in doing so, checking against what we can experience during the day. Then it will come ...)

Science comes to the idea of wavelength (which, however, it does not apply to *all* light phenomena) through theories and experiments, some of which already have *made assumptions* about the nature of light and colour. We can, however, come to other models for light and colour through other theories and other experiments. Yet throughout all these, two facts remain as though *given along with creation*: the yellow process and the blue process come to manifestation, they *appear*, through quite consistent juxtapositions of light and darkness; and they *always* appear when the conditions are there—this is the 'primal phenomenon' of colour.

Green, made through bringing yellow and blue together, either in a prism or in other ways, becomes the innocent victim of man's materialistic mind when he calculates for her a wavelength, justified by a spectrometer and some algebra, which are man-made too (and very valuable tools they are). But they do not explain Nature's best dress! Is she (green) not truly born when yellow is lightened by the conditions that reveal blue, or blue darkened by the conditions that reveal yellow? And yet green, when she emerges, is darker in different ways than both yellow and cyan!

No, this is not a mistake. We think of blue as a dark colour, but it is conjured up through lightening of the darkness. We think of yellow as a light colour, but it shows through as a darkening of the light. Thus green is primarily a merging of two processes until they *balance* and neutralize each other. Lightening and darkening work together doubly to create green, to let green *appear*. And if the violet and the red, where the two colour processes are at their most intense, are brought together instead of the blue and yellow, they make way for magenta. (A black strip seen through a prism illustrates this.)

Rudolf Steiner, in lectures on colour,[23] described two families of colours: those that shine out and those that portray. He develops green as the *image* of what is alive as the greens of plants. This is not 'life' itself, for that is invisible, but its image in the world of matter—hence 'green is the dead image of the living'. In a comparable way, he describes magenta as the 'living image of the soul', as when cheeks reveal a healthy, well-constituted person.

When beholding magenta in the sky as described above, one does easily have the experience of being face-to-face with the countenance of a spiritual being.

We owe to science its clarity and exactness: intellect is used at its best here. But the human spirit must remember that science produces theorems—from the Greek, literally concepts through which we *see* the world in order to understand it. The world secrets, however, are only unlocked by the human soul (how else?). Simply by clearing the eye and mind from shadows of intellect one can find that nature answers us by showing little surprises, phenomena which are just what we need for our next step in true thought. When the full colour process works down into the sense world we are given green; when it opens itself upwards towards the spirit we see magenta, the colour gateway into the soul world.

To sum up the 'science' derived from these two meditations: The 'primal phenomenon' of colour is the pair of coloured boundaries at the transition from dark to light: yellow-orange-red and cyan-blue-violet. They are part of the very fabric of creation, natural law. Under certain given conditions they must, and do, appear. In creation language, they have been put there by the Creative Divinity through its highest co-workers (Seraphim and Cherubim) as part of the divine Idea of the world.

Pink and green, on the other hand, are *secondary* phenomena. They do not rank with the 'eternal' nature of yellow and blue but are not thereby lesser in value; for they are born out of the now, the present happenings that involve us as observers and experiencers. They are part of the *dynamic* of creation, the work—again in the language of creation—of middle-ranking spirit beings, the Elohim (in anthroposophy, Spirits of Form, who form the outer creation and Man, out of the raw material of Cherubim, Seraphim and Thrones, beings of substance, sense-quality and will).

So just by looking at the sky we can gradually see the outer signs of two distinct realms of creation: science (blue and yellow) and art and craft (green and magenta). When we then wonder at this and take it into our soul to let our spirit be nourished and lifted up by it, we engage the third realm of spiritual beings, Angels and Archangels, those who have to do with the inner part of Man. Through our observation and pondering we have engaged with all the ranks that stand and move between us and God. This may contribute to answering the modern riddle that we are discussing in this Michaelmas chapter: 'Who like God?' But a science that stays with treating a secondary phenomenon (green) as a primary one, by saying that light contains (how can it—is it a jug of some kind?) seven colours, including green, will never be able to reply sensibly because it bypasses the one who both observes and experiences, Man.

Biblical context

Michael is often represented artistically bearing the Scales, the zodiacal sign of Libra, September–October. We can say to ourselves: balance your life between flying too high and being dragged down and fixed to what is earthly, that you not be 'lukewarm' (Rev. 3:16). Know how to aim high, be consequential and thorough but do not become a 'type', a role player. Be more than a '*hum*an being', of whatever gender, created out of earth (*hum-* = earth). Rudolf Steiner describes in *Occult Science* that the first human being was an expression of those evolutionary stages preceding Earth evolution proper: Adam, who was made out of earth—the humus* as it was then—and created by Jehovah (and originally male-female). Do not remain as you were in the Garden of Eden, 'but stand upright, lift up your heads' (Luke 21:28). That is what is contained in the word Man, the one who can look up to the spiritual (cf. Greek *anthropos*, the one who looks up), who can look up to 'Spirit Self' or '*Man*as', which was described by Rudolf Steiner[24] as the next stage of evolution in which we become social beings after filling out with warmth the new-found ego-ness, and which left to itself in its oneness becomes 'all alone and ever more shall be so' ('I'll sing you one-oh'). Strictly speaking, according to its etymology, the 'human' or earthly being (cf. *humus*), cannot be like God. He/she is restricted to being human, of the earth, until the seed of divinity opens within and raises him/her up.

Meditative pictures

1. Michael overcomes the dragon to save the child of the heavenly Woman (Rev. 12:1–9). This is the original Michael-dragon picture. No weaponry is seen; the dragon is not slain—he fights but is cast out of the spiritual world onto the Earth, at least partly because he wants to consume the Spirit Man, born of the Sun. When I struggle to bring something new to birth, it will be attacked. Take courage that the spiritual world is stronger than evil and can put it in its place. We can do this too if we choose, but keep our eyes open for this evil, for its place of work is now here on Earth and its power can sometimes be put to good use, as when St Benedict makes the devil push the wheelbarrow for building his church, as a punishment for putting hindrances in his

* Humus is that kind of soil produced out of healthy *decay* processes that provides a healthy basis for *new* growth. The creation story of anthroposophy sees a comparison here: evolution from pre-earthly aeons went through a healthy process of dissolution to reappear as a medium out of which human origins emerged. It was only later that this man of earth received divine breath into him, to raise him up to become 'Man'.

way. In our time we find that forces that can be destructive can also be used to help people and save lives, for example in electronic hospital equipment. The dumper truck is the modern wheelbarrow, but for the driver ear protection is advisable!

2. In a Russian legend, Michael could not believe that the innocent Jesus Christ could be crucified,[25] but Christ chides him and instructs him, and he becomes the first of the spiritual beings to grasp that the World Creator would begin a new creation (old and new Adam, 1 Cor. 15:45) with Man, by overcoming death. Many who have tried to work artistically know of that death-moment when everything has become a mess—it can either herald failure or become the beginning of the real work!
3. And, thirdly, Michael converts his sword into a lyre, the instrument that works on the heart to harmonize thinking, feeling and doing (Polish legend, source unknown). Man, remember that all your modern (technological) works need to be counterbalanced therapeutically with harmony and all artistic disciplines be applied therapeutically as well.
4. In the Old Testament: Exod. 34:29–35, the shining countenance of Moses; Num. 12:5–8, God speaks to Moses face to face; Jos. 5:13–15, the commander of the army of the Lord; and 2 Kings 6:14–17, chariots of fire. And in the New Testament: Matt. 22:1–14; Matt. 25:1–13; Matt. 25:14–30, images of michaelic attitudes and dispositions; Eph. 6:10–17, the armour of God; Rev. 3:1–6, tasks of a Michael age; and especially Rev. 12:1–9, Michael defeating the dragon.
5. Egyptian legends of Horus and Set and their battles and intrigues. These appear to be about good against evil; but they can also be read as the struggle for balance between order and disorder. Pharaohs who did balance them became able to inaugurate a new surge of development.
6. The *Bhagavadgita* with its war for emancipation from blood ties and Arjuna's vision of the countenance of God also provide substance for the background life of this festival.

Prayer

In the light of the above, it would be appropriate and helpful to pray at this time for leaders of state, of institutions—those who need ideals and the imagination and ability to carry them through. They need good judgement, insight, balance and courage. They need to see the *human being*, whom they rightly serve, and not lose him from the picture through modern pressures, temptations and ambitions, but raise him to be truly Man. One can also pray for members of one's community, society, even nation, for their well-being, but mainly for their understanding of each other in mutual roles (family, nation, to the great family of mankind). What I hope for myself can I hope for others on all these levels? (This is the progression of our relationship with our guardian angel through our 'Folk Spirit' or Nation Spirit—an archangel—to the Spirit of the Age. And this is relevant at Michaelmas: 'St Michael *and All Angels*'). One can pray also for spiritual leaders, of Churches, of faiths, also of non-religious spiritual movements, that they avoid dogmas and the authority of mere position in favour of inner strength of vision born of the effort to understand those they serve.

And, for oneself, pray for courage to stand before danger and the unknown in one's life or before the known and dreaded; for honesty to oneself about one's feelings; to admit to despair, anger, antipathy, scorn and pride. Pray also for contentment, reverence, respect and peace. Pray for power to put into practice what we feel to be our best deed in a situation, for such deeds are good seeds for future growth.

How? Sit quietly, bring the body to repose, the soul to stillness and the mind to a clear emptiness. Visualize the highest being you can and let your heart warm your best thoughts about the content of your prayer—at first crystal clear—so they dissolve upwards and outwards to fill the Being of the Universe. Sometimes you will feel: this was a happening in that very universe, a true communication in Will with its spirit.

Something else relating to prayer: the resolution of the life of elemental beings

Now, do you recall the journey we have made through the four elements and their indwelling beings? We tried to penetrate certain sense perceptions in such a way that doors opened, largely by capturing a special gesture in nature that moves us into a world beyond, illuminated traditionally by poets and painters but now methodically in our quest for ways of leading nature out beyond herself through our own fire of creativity. We opened up the possibility of experiencing these beings of the elements as cooperators in our festival activities, even up to the point of connecting 'bright ideas' with those of the element of warmth. So where does this journey take us next? 'Elemental' means 'of the elements'. These beings are also called 'elementary' beings because they *emerge* out of a particular element, use it for their 'body', then, at the end of their term of activity, dissolve back into the element from which they came. But they, like us, are not only their body; they have a soul too, albeit an 'elemental one', not backed up by an ego or an animal soul (or group soul) that would make for a more permanent existence. This soul element, however, although transitory, does have a destiny, which we shall look at now.

One consistent feature of folk tales involving fairy folk or other elemental beings is that they seek involvement with humankind—for better or worse. Sometimes they are mischievous or evil from the outset; sometimes they merely deliver evil to those human beings who mistreat them through pride, meanness or greed. We see, therefore, that they can give—or take away. For *themselves*, however, they require something from us, maybe the traditional bread or porridge on the doorstep or maybe something more substantial. Anthroposophy tells us that nature spirits have a neutral destiny as long as they remain completely within the frontiers of nature but that the moment there is human contact this destiny changes radically.[26] Their future, once their role within nature is fulfilled, is determined by whether they have been positively regarded and valued by us or not. This too is related in folklore; and children used to say that a fairy died every time someone declared they did not believe in them. When we see a plant, we may view it for the pleasure it gives us or its economic value to us, but also just see it for what it is. This means how it grows, what its gestures are, and how an individual specimen derives its special individual qualities out of the archetype. This bestows on the plant an objective soul-spiritual component that does implicitly belong to it but is not incorporated *in* it within the natural order. Man has his physical body, life (etheric) body, soul and spirit all united, during the waking state, within the earthly world. In sleep his soul and spirit loose themselves from their bodily components and move in soul and spirit worlds, usually unconsciously. Then the physical and life bodies are on a par with the plant. For the plant's physical and life bodies live on the Earth; their soul and spirit live outside them, just touching from above in the blossom. But the waking human being that becomes conscious of the plant creates for it its *full stature, within* the earthly realm, within the fourfold working of the elemental beings. (The animal is midway: it contains its own soul (anima) on the earthly plane but its spirit lives in the soul world within a 'group soul', that is, a single being (or 'species') that extends down into each of its animals and withdraws again when it dies.

Thus the four kingdoms of nature express outwardly the four parts of the human being; and the four elemental beings relate to those too. The gnomes help in the skilful use of tools, the undines in life processes, the sylphs engage with our souls in delight or woe and the fire-spirits can be our helpers in spirit and thought. This aids our understanding as to how we can give them a future. One must remember that they are in every process within a particular element and then see how this works. We may often be rewarded in this by seeing something that we had not noticed before or seeing an especially rare phenomenon that contributes to our research in an unexpected and gratifying way. When such a thing can come about through our loving efforts in this realm, the elemental being in question, after its release from the old order, is taken up into the realm of the Archangel Michael. This means that the soul content of this being, acquired in its sojourn in its elemental body, is absorbed into the special soul nature of this spirit-guide of the present time, Michael. The good fruits of its encounter with the human spirit are thereby carried to him also.

Here is an elementary spirit:

whatever part of the greater whole it has inhabited
—whether in nature outside us or nature inside us . . .
that part is united in soul and spirit to the one that was missing,
that was only perceived and created on a higher plane
through our own mental-spiritual activity.
Something is therefore created new
that contains an important ingredient not to be found in nature
and therefore will not perish with nature.
We have again been part of the 'second creation'.

You could imagine something like this, although nature is manifold and her processes do not all synchronize with the outer seasons as here portrayed. As the natural phenomena die away or fade out of existence, the elementary beings enchanted into them during the First Creation are released from nature and rise up as nature falls away. They rise up, borne aloft with myriads of others by those earth forces from the St John's Tide period that have been transmuted into golden rays by the new Earth Spirit of the Resurrection. They are then embraced by the heavenly mantle of responsibility that Michael bears through the task he has accepted in leading mankind along spirit-guided paths out of materialism again. Each of these beings loses itself in the fabric of that mantle and is transmuted into spirit. Then, as Michaelmas passes over through November towards Advent, we may imagine in feeling that the mantle has lifted away still higher and reaches the periphery of our ken. It becomes the deep, dark blue of the cosmic embrace, the Mantle of Mary.

In the event that mankind defaults on this possibility, however, the beings of the elements will have to receive the opposite destiny, namely to become elementals of sub-nature, which includes ingredients of technology such as electronic equipment, certain chemically based substances and certain viral or mass hysterical phenomena. We get an idea of the feeling of this when we have tried our best in something and been rejected or scorned. The reactions that arise within us are sometimes ones we do not wish to acknowledge as our own. The good destiny of redemption, however, makes it possible for Man to transform these, just as we have explored ways of liberating those of nature. Yet *their* overcoming is a true exercise in love and clearly brings redemption, for it defuses an ill and creates a good.

Just as our thoughts are able to reach into the spiritual world, so elemental beings are the spirit that reaches into *our* world. Behind them stand and move the higher beings that engender them, call them into existence out of cosmic soul substance and send them into the bodies of elemental ether to carry out their task.[27] From our side, behind each deed of redemptive or creative love stands the one who also stands behind Michael, whose countenance he is, the main motif of this chapter.

In the realm in which these worlds overlap, the worlds of sense perception and the ideas developed from it,
and in the loving, knowing imaginative activity that we bring to bear in causing them to overlap—
. . . in that overlap (and only there) arises full reality.
Perception is placed with understanding into its full context
(which includes its ultimate causes and the beings both behind its genesis and within its nature)
(including our inner perceptions too);

And our inner life is brought to fulfilment when its consequential, willed deed is carried out from it in freedom.

The festive expression of this is depicted in the Apocalypse (Rev. 19) as New Heaven and New Earth, the New Jerusalem, that descends from God out of Heaven adorned as a bride. The old Earth is made up of natural and human phenomena, the old Heaven their spiritual origins and causes and our own enhanced thought world. The new Heaven-and-Earth, the New Jerusalem, is the 'Second Creation', part of which we co-created by working through this cycle of festivals.

Contemplation of nature—in northern and southern continents

All these areas in which nature can be integrated into our festival can equally well apply in countries where it is not all autumn winds and golden leaves and chestnuts!

For Rudolf Steiner, celebrating the Michaelmas festival to express the quality of the times was all important. He presented it as a challenge to his pupils to find the spirit through inner work, which meant the study of his contributions to anthroposophy and the efforts at concentration and meditation as a strengthening of thought that would result in the opening up of the spiritual world within the human mind, and to express this in festive form—a true challenge for imagination and technique! He gave a Michaelmas meditation which helps us understand that this festival is independent of the outer season: 'meteoric iron' (referring to the meteor showers of August). This meditation looks at iron as one of the basic raw materials of the Earth; although it has been made into a kind of foundation for the modern world in its utilitarian quality, it actually has an extraterrestrial origin. (Anthroposophy presents the picture that iron has entered the Earth from the solar system early in its evolution as well as in the now smaller quantities that fall as meteorites.) He then challenges us to look at the qualities that are associated with the *spiritual* origin of iron and therefore lead on to a *spiritual* goal. Then it will bring a salutary wholeness into human life! Pure iron is softer than cast iron or steel. If you hold a piece in your hand for a while it becomes easier to enter into the imagination of the pure iron in the blood that strengthens our will, gives force to our speaking and quickens the processes of our spirit. For Steiner, therefore, the Michaelmas motif is totally independent of outer nature but illustrative of the possibility (or need) to take outer nature and spiritualize her in the way that this book is trying to describe.

For children, of course, local nature *should* be used, for they are still growing *into* nature. But for adults, true humanity lies in rising above our nature yet not above responsibility for it. We should be growing *out* of her, so the festival achieves greater depth when the purely seasonal aspect is balanced by elements valid the world over. This is a quite vexing point, for as children we have quite rightly grown up close to nature in our festivals and we might here recall what was discussed in the first two chapters about festivals which are geographically anchored in the Northern Hemisphere.

Creating your festival

Self-knowledge is a good start: to become aware of our assumptions about our own character and our standing with others. Are these borne out by the messages we receive from them or from life? Where is more modesty or humility needed? Where could we bring in a balancing quality to one of our favourite attributes? Where do we catch ourselves criticizing in our partner just those faults that are ours? And where would a few sparks off a heavenly sword make a bit of difference? Or are we content to miss opportunities through laziness, cowardice or lack of vision? And what about our view of the world? Do we believe what is written in learned sounding articles? Can we perceive the assumptions about Man on which they are founded? What is the inner message to the 'inner human being who is like God' that a play or film really tells? Where are modern heroes on the scale between animal and angel? Can we spot the truth or the error? And in films and advertisements there are often allusions to themes from the deeper mysteries of, say, Christianity or the mysteries of evil—not just the idea and picture content but the compelling force that it applies to us. What does our common sense say about them? For example, can we sort out the real message of a comedy or a serious play about a modern dilemma or tell who is for the good and who for the two types of evil in a modern fantasy film? This can sometimes be difficult. The Michaelmas task is to balance them, the hot and the cold, the *diabolic* or exhilaratingly confusing with the *satanic* or sclerotically destructive. Steiner uses the names Lucifer and Ahriman for the cosmic beings behind these tendencies. Lucifer is the light-bringer, the inspirer to freedom, art and an outward-goer; Ahriman is 'the father of lies and murderer from the beginning' (John 8:44), and an isolationist, the leader of technology. They have their valid place in the universe and serve Man if he can remain free of their extreme tendencies by balancing them off against one another in life, stepping through the midst with poise. A final question, a most important one: can I identify needs in the world which call me to develop new strengths or talents to be able to apply myself, to go beyond myself for their sake?

So how can this be formed into a festive event? We can start with this call of the world—what is wanted that we cannot yet achieve—and try to express it in a real deed, something that at once *portrays* it and makes a start on *answering* it. The scope is wide but, having chosen it, it needs to be inspired by a true picture of the human being—not the higher ape who should never get ill or be troubled by questions of conscience, but one who is learning to decide each action on its own merits, bravely taking the consequences, learning from mistakes and resolving to try again, out of the sense of responsibility to oneself and the world. And try yet again! Give the actual event an artistic *form*, i.e. a clear motif running all the way through a structure that has opening and closing items relating to one another; or include a poem, a piece of writing or music (live!). A play could be created or a picture (of Michael or of the heavenly Woman) hung as a centrepiece or backdrop. Wherever possible be inventive, and include a social dimension that gives everyone the opportunity to encounter each other in just that part of themselves where the above themes are relevant (in a little drama selected for the occasion, in small conversation groups or simply over a cup of tea!). Kindle the feeling that it is *always* worth trying again, as long as each attempt has utilized the previous failure but also adds a new thought.

In a lecture in Berlin on 23 May 1923, Rudolf Steiner remarked, 'The Michaelmas festival is about doing things to change life and culture in the future, according to ideas and ideals gleaned from anthroposophy. It is where things are dying, whether in nature (agriculture etc.) or in human affairs (culture, social order, etc.) that the spirit may enter in this way. The spirit of this festival is therefore a future oriented one, in contrast to Christmas and Easter and other festivals which are based upon something that happened in the past, even if the purpose of the festival is to make them again present.'

To close this festival season, which can extend until 30 October (prior to Halloween), reflect on what has lived throughout the month. Make a harvest of its fruits. What has ripened through the celebrations, through one's prayers and meditations? Where have new impulses made themselves felt? Grasping these, with awareness in a warm human heart and with a will to serve, opens the way to the next festival time: All Saints' Day and All Souls' Day.

Summary

The message of Michaelmas is to strive first of all for an inspired vision of the human being as separate from, and more advanced than, animals and plants—but therefore responsible for them, and indeed for making the best out of all that is in the world yet holding its evils in check. Also, it leads us to grasp ever more deeply what happened at the crucifixion and resurrection of Jesus Christ, and to heal where human will is lamed through personal passions or social malformations. When this lives within us, we can let nature take her downward course, for she will live on in us, upwards.

In the paragraph on Prayer (p. 112), we put forth the possibility of experiencing through thinking about, feeling bonded with and doing something about the world problems that have touched us. Through this experience of having 'done something about something' in the context of the whole universe, we can develop the idea of God as a Being who advances in evolution as we advance.

The Michael question begins to be answered.

13
ALL SAINTS' AND ALL SOULS' DAYS

1 and 2 November

Motif

At Michaelmas we reminded ourselves that the full festival title is St Michael and All Angels. The activity of grateful reflection upon an inner harvest could perhaps open our soul to the gaze and feelings of 'all angels', notably our guardian spirit-companion, tutor and guide through the ages who, with all the others of its kind, will receive our thoughts, prayers, feelings and intentions, and integrate them (if they are realistic ones) with the orderly progress of spiritual worlds.

So if on the 'e'en' (31 October) of All-Hallows we picture these soul-fruits of Michaelmas rising towards the spiritual beings who guide humanity, we can visualize how the 'saints' (those human beings who are able to work with them) are now addressed by our will for the future.

What is meant by 'saints' and 'souls' is explained under the section *Biblical Context* below.

Nature

November is a severe month. Leaden skies are like a shroud to the world, the colour is going and winds blow leaves hither and thither. Nature has withdrawn gloriously. The year is closing down and life descends into the realm below.

Biblical context

An aspect of this is depicted in the Apocalypse (Rev. 5:8 and 8:3) where angels use our prayers as their incense before God at the altar in the spiritual world. Is not this turning from the *reflections* upon the month of Michaelmas to the *supplications* towards the God of man's future a better form of preparation for All Saints' than the mammonic spread of ugliness over the last few years at Hallowe'en? Is it not more wholesome by far to remember that evil is banished or tamed from within by beauty and morality? One can still dress a child as a witch aesthetically and humorously without using all the plastic trappings from the shops which simply perpetrate forceful images of the inhuman and anti-human. (Not 'Who is like God?' but 'Who is like the Beast'—Rev. 13:4). By 'saints' are meant not only those canonized by Churches but those who have been able during their earthly lives to embody certain of the redemptive attributes of the divine will, whether this was manifested in a particular religion or through their own essential humanity. This is not a matter of having had visions, carried out healings or being visited by supernatural phenomena but by being a living witness to true humanity to such a degree that others could come more into their own humanity in their presence. We need here to distinguish between humanity and humanism. Humanism emphasizes the earthly and 'humus' aspect of man that we have referred to before; *humanity* adds to humanism the human striving for the spirit. To realize eternal being in every moment of earthly life, especially within the context of a striving community—this is a foundation for the awakening of the same faculty after death, the faculty of 'sainthood'. Such people are the mediators, those mentioned in some of the books published in the last 20 years on post-mortem life as helping newcomers orientate themselves, healing the trauma of dying but also helping ray down grace to the world of those still incarnate. There are many more of these than are to be found in the calendar! They feel Christ in themselves, not only the Christ of the Christian religion but Christ as the radiant source of all the life of the universe.

The circle widens on 2 November to include All Souls', all the souls in the afterlife who had striven on this side to realize their own freely chosen ideals, however modestly, for they too have the power after death to influence benignly the affairs of Earth including our own spiritual activities. We can pay special attention in this month to where our real will is taking us and how chance events change our planned day into the day that made us live (or die), for this sometimes reveals the inworking of those who have died.

Within the totality of all those who have died are thus to be found 'all souls' who in life cared for something beyond themselves. They have more light and can find each other better in the spiritual world. Amongst *them* again are those who practised on Earth a devotion to the spirit in a *religious* way. They reach communion in still higher spheres. Then there are those whose religion transcended all limits of race or creed: their heart is like the Sun. Thereby their heart could be a place for Christ: they are the 'saints', having the capacity to help others both in spirit and on Earth.

Meditative pictures

We referred above to incense mentioned in the Book of Revelation in connection with the saints. There, a spiritual picture is given that shows incense to be that ritual substance which depicts how a prayer works. What is the connection between prayer and incense? What we *see* is the smoke rising and spreading out. But what is it that brings about the smoke?

The plants from which incense substances come grow in very hot climates where there is much bright sunlight. The plant absorbs the brightness of the light into itself. Later the resin is extracted and this is burned on glowing charcoal. We therefore need two things in order to pray. First we need light, that is, far-reaching thoughts about the world, making things clear. Secondly we need warmth, warmth of heart, caring for what we are going to pray about. When we then use *will-power* to bring these two ingredients together our *whole* soul is engaged: our thoughts, our feelings and our doing (will), under the rulership of our higher self.

Prayer

We are now able to pray both *for* those who have died and *through them* to higher powers about the things that speak to us as needs.

Out of the mood of Michaelmas, we think especially of the needs of situations to lead positively into the future, to bear good fruit. So in our prayers we focus on that: redemption and fruitfulness.

Then our prayer rises, accompanied, we may imagine, by our guardian angel, first to 'all saints' and 'all souls', then to the higher beings at the archetypal spiritual altar, who lend them their own power to send them further. They enter the spiritual economy of the universe, to return as blessing, charged with the divine powers of grace and fortune, to rectify the situations we cared about—or even others of which we were ignorant.

Contemplation of nature—in northern and southern continents

It is often well into autumn before we become aware again of birdsong after the comparative stillness of late summer. One of the first is the robin. The more we get to know the robin, the more special does he seem to be to us. He exhibits a confidence, a curiosity and even friendliness. The robin will come to eat through an open kitchen window if patiently encouraged. And the robin has a unique way of looking at one, quite differently from other birds. One almost feels addressed as an equal! His mannerisms give us the impression of a friend and he can open our minds and hearts to just this realm beyond the threshold. His song of course comes from there, and when we are thinking of those who have died and he appears and sings, the experience can certainly make a deep impression upon us. In other parts of the world there may be other birds to play this role.

There is nothing scientific about this: it is just the quality of the *experience* of the robin that is so special that we are moved inwardly to be open to the world beyond. Do we not always feel somehow grateful when he appears? In soul we talk to our own angel, but in nature it is the robin who reminds us of this in outer picture and experience.

Creating your festival

Many nations celebrate their war-dead in this month. And we can, fortified by 'saints' and 'souls' at the beginning of the month, extend our prayers, thoughts and feelings to *all* who have died, and now especially those in tragic circumstances, for we no longer need feel isolated in any attempt to succour them. All angels, 'saints' and 'souls' surround them in their soul darkness with wraps of light, glowing warmly, which will one day permeate them, enlighten them and give them healing. Our efforts in this direction do indeed also give sustenance to all these beings of the spiritual world. Again, we can use our full artistic freedom to create an outer form for this in our home.

Within the tradition that the festive year begins with Advent, this festival closes it.

Summary

November is under the sign of Scorpio, calling for the positive response of the strengthened human soul to the sting of our fallen nature. It links our spirit to the rising Eagle who heralds the power awakening within us to care selflessly for the true being of the other (in anthroposophy called the Spirit Self or Manas).[28] The eternal spirit of the returning circle of the festivals and their healing of the whole Earth bears this future towards us.

14
A COLOUR EPILOGUE
Red

We have tried at various points of this book to look at colour phenomena through natural observation of the genesis of yellow and blue in the atmosphere. We have seen how these colours open up into *families* of colours: yellow, orange and red, then cyan, blue and violet. We have also seen how these two families meet below in green and intensify towards each other above in what has loosely been called magenta. We have watched them act and react in various settings of nature to make up the world that we see: Sun, clouds, sky, trees, shadows and the earth.

As an after-image of this book of festivals in which we try to lead nature to transcend herself by applying our spiritual, creative inventiveness, let us look imaginatively at this quality of magenta. We can see that here too, as with yellow and blue, there is a red *family*. Here we find certain kinds of pink (the kind containing no white). Magenta is quite a strong colour but in its family there is also a lighter shade, lighter than both violet and red. This is often called peach blossom or incarnate, the colour of healthy rosy cheeks. So magenta-red unfolds itself into five shades lying between red and violet: pink-red, rose-magenta, peach blossom, violet-rose and rose-violet. Notice that the yellow and blue families are linear, each 'parent' becoming darker, whereas this one unfolds itself outwards from itself or inwards from its red or violet neighbours. The red-magenta parent is no longer to be seen.

Let us make a circle of these colours. At the bottom is green, to the left of it is a light yellow and to the right a light blue. Beyond these we place an orange and a blue, then a red and a violet respectively. The two families show their earthly progeny, green. But between the warm red and the violet we now let the magenta open up into this other colour range. They are all lighter than the red and the violet. Now imagine that at that point, the space between red and violet, the circle turns over itself to become a figure of eight, the lower part containing the seven colours and the upper part the five lighter members of the red family, born out of the magenta.

In these two arrangements we have the two aspects of red: the red-magenta as a *shining out* of the force of life; and the lighter range of five colours which can then be imagined (and, with practice, seen) as approaching us from beyond the sense world as a *picture*, variations of the colour of a healthy countenance.

Whose?

I hope that by working with the cycle of the year through its Christian festivals we may gradually come to the same impression: that the after-image of the earthly celebration of these festivals comes towards us from the other side like a living spiritual countenance: the being whose life is revealed in their archetypes and who responds to and joins in our work.

NOTES

Biblical quotations in the text are from the Revised Standard Version or, where stated, rendered from Greek by the author.

1. See Ormond Edwards, *A New Chronology of the Gospels*, Floris Books, Edinburgh 1986.
2. Rudolf Steiner, *Theosophy* (GA 9), trans. M. Cotterell & A.P. Shepherd, Rudolf Steiner Press, 2005.
3. Rudolf Steiner, *Knowledge of the Higher Worlds: How is it Achieved?* (GA 10), trans. D.S. Osmond & C. Davy, Rudolf Steiner Press, 2004.
4. Rudolf Steiner, *The Stages of Higher Knowledge* (GA 12), trans. L. Monges & F. McKnight, SteinerBooks, Great Barrington, MA, 2009. First published under the title *The Gates of Knowledge*, this short book is a sequel to *Knowledge of the Higher Worlds*.
5. Rudolf Steiner, *Occult Science: An Outline* (GA 13), trans. George & Mary Adams, Rudolf Steiner Press, 2005.
6. Rudolf Steiner, *Spiritual Beings in the Heavenly Bodies and the Kingdoms of Nature* (GA 136), Anthroposophic Press, Hudson, NY, 1992.
7. Rudolf Steiner, *Harmony of the Creative Word* (GA 230), Lecture 7, Rudolf Steiner Press, 2001.
8. Rudolf Steiner, *The Four Seasons and the Archangels* (GA 229), lecture of 12 October 1923, Rudolf Steiner Press, 2008.
9. Rudolf Steiner, *Calendar of the Soul* (from GA 40), trans. Owen Barfield, Rudolf Steiner Press, 2006.
10. Ormond Edwards, *A New Chronology of the Gospels*.
11. Ibid.
12. See Steiner, *Harmony of the Creative Word*, Lectures 7–9.
13. See in particular R. Steiner, *Spiritual Beings in the Heavenly Bodies and the Kingdoms of Nature* and *Harmony of the Creative Word*.
14. Ormond Edwards, *A New Chronology of the Gospels*.
15. Ibid.
16. Steiner, *Occult Science*, Section V, Part 2.
17. Angelus Silesius (1624–77), *Der Cherubinische Wandersmann* (The Cherubinic Pilgrim).
18. On gnomes, see Steiner, *Harmony of the Creative Word*.
19. For an introduction to the etheric body, see Steiner, *Theosophy*, Chapter 1, 'The Essential Nature of Man'.
20. Ibid.
21. See Steiner, *The Four Seasons and the Archangels*, 'The St John's Imagination' (lecture of 12 October 1923).

22. Two excellent books on these subjects are: Fred Schaaf, *Wonders of the Sky*, Dover Publications, Mineola, NY, 1983; M. Minnaert, *The Nature of Light and Colour*, Dover Publications, Mineola, NY, 1954.
23. Rudolf Steiner, *Colour* (GA 291), Lecture 2, Rudolf Steiner Press, 2005.
24. Steiner, *Theosophy*.
25. A Russian legend, from Nora Stein's collection of Michael traditions (in German), 1929.
26. See Rudolf Steiner, *Michaelmas and the Soul Forces of Man* (from GA 223), Lecture 2 (28 September 1923), Anthroposophic Press, Hudson, NY, 1982. (Originally published under the title *Anthroposophy and the Human Gemüt*.)
27. See Steiner, *The Spiritual Beings in the Heavenly Bodies and Kingdoms of Nature*.
28. Steiner, *Theosophy*.